D1205025

THERE'S MORE BODIES OUT THERE

The True Story of
a Mafia Associate and a Cop
Who Emerge as Suspected Serial Killers

Rick Porrello

To Susan –
With fond regards
and best wishes,
Rick P.
11·29·22

Next
Hat
Press,
LLC

Published by Next Hat Press, LLC
P.O. Box 23
Novelty, OH 44072
www.rickporrello.com
info@rickporrello.com

Copyright © 2023 Rick Porrello

All Rights Reserved
No part of this book may be reproduced, stored in a retrieval system,
or transmitted in any form, by any means, including mechanical,
electronic, photocopying, recording, or otherwise, without the
prior written permission of the publisher, except by a reviewer
who wishes to quote brief passages in connection with a review
written for inclusion in a magazine, newspaper, or broadcast.

Cover design by JD&J Design, LLC, and Rick Porrello
Interior design by Integrative Ink

Library of Congress Control Number: 2022910814
Publisher's Cataloging-in-Publication
(Provided by Cassidy Cataloguing Services, Inc.)

Names: Porrello, Rick, author.
Title: There's more bodies out there : the true story of a Mafia associate and a
            cop who emerge as suspected serial killers / Rick Porrello.
Description: Novelty, OH: Next Hat Press, [2022] | Includes bibliographical
                 references and index.
Identifiers: ISBN: 9780966250817 (trade paperback) | 9780966250800
                 (ebook) | LCCN: 2022910814
Subjects: LCSH: Henkel, Richard E. | Serial murderers--United States--
               History--20th century. | Serial murderers--British Columbia--
               History--20th century. | Mafia--Pennsylvania--Pittsburgh--
               History--20th century. | Police--Pennsylvania--Pittsburgh--
               History--20th century. | LCGFT: True crime stories.
Classification: LCC: HV6248.H425 P67 2022 | DDC: 364.15230973--dc23

Dedicated to the memory of
Deborah Kelber Burge Gentile

CONTENTS

AUTHOR'S NOTE

This is a true story. My sources include written correspondence with Richard Henkel, government reports, newspaper
articles, books, and personal interviews. On rare occasions, I
formulated conclusions based on conjecture or edited quotes for
clarity. Endnotes provide additional information.

All persons not convicted of crimes are presumed innocent.

Rick Porrello

ACKNOWLEDGMENTS

Thank you to the Pittsburgh Post-Gazette, the former Pittsburgh Press, Pittsburgh Action 4 News, and their reporters, including the following, for their extensive coverage of the characters and events in this story. William Allan, Jr., Robert Baird, Lee Bowman, Stuart Brown, Ann Butler, Eleanor Chute, Jim Cuddy, Jr., John Downing, Stu Emry, J. Kenneth Evans. Debra Fox, Jim Gallagher, Joyce Gemperlein, Connie Giel, Rich Gigler, Dan Giovannitti, Joe Grata, Jack Grochot, Don Hopey, Thomas M. Hritz, Fritz Huysman, Gabriel Ireton, Robert Johnson, Matthew Kennedy, Earl Kohnfelder, Carmen J. Lee, Toni Locy, Adam Lynch, Charles Lynch, Lorraine Macklin, Susan Mannella, Paul Maryniak, William Mausteller, James McCarron, William McCloskey, Mike Moyle, David Nilsson, Torsten Ove, Carole Patton, Edwina Rankin, Doug Root, Alvin Rosensweet, Martin Smith, Mary Stolberg, Roger Stuart, Harry Tkach, Geoffrey Tomb, Tim Vercellotti, Chet Wade, Lawrence Walsh, Linda S. Wilson, and William Wisser.

Thank you to the Allegheny County Medical Examiner and Coroner, Allegheny County Police Dept., Anonymous, the Carnegie Library of Pittsburgh, Johnny Chechitelli, Phil Christopher, Burt Cifrulak, Kelsea Collins, Thomas M. Fitzgerald,

Paul Maryniak, Kim W. Riester, James Ross, and Jeffrey H. Schwartz.

Thank you to my editors, Eve Porinchak and Kim Bookless.

Special thank you to Chief Robert Payne of the Edgewood, PA Police Department for sharing his memories and collection of the Richard Henkel case from his time as an Allegheny County Police Department homicide detective.

INTRODUCTION

Under a convincing veneer of normalcy lurks the real Richard Henkel. Federal parole authorities deemed the incarcerated bank robber psychologically stable and ready to make positive contributions to society.

They got it wrong.

Henkel operated within the underworld of the 1970s—the well-entrenched Mafia with their interstate connections and a loose network of drug dealers, burglars, and pimps. Ex-convict Jack Siggson and police officer Gary Small found him to be loyal. Dick would never rat out a pal. Though he might kill him. Or her.

In the background of Richard Henkel's world were the massage parlor "rub and tug" sex shops that politicians tried in vain to regulate and mob-connected operators would kill to control. The girls were easy marks. Most came from troubled childhoods.

Some of the women in Richard's life also had rocky backgrounds. He met their needs, be it cash or a place to live. Suzanne Dixon became his fiancée. Her best friend—like a little sister, really—was Sasha Scott. Richard may have saved Sasha's life, but she did not recognize the twists in his plot. For Debbie Gentile, Richard provided employment, and she believed she was emerging from her longtime financial struggles.

Richard Henkel's victims were numerous but not random. He was not the stereotypical serial killer who worked alone and slaughtered for twisted motives of sexual pleasure or power. And Richard's victims usually were not without their own sins.

There's More Bodies Out There is the always compelling, often tense, and sometimes maddening story of one of the most dangerous con artists in US history, those who fell victim to his venom, and the lawmen who persevered to lift the veil and serve justice.

PART 1

Lead Characters:

Richard Henkel
Nick Delucia: prostitution network boss
George Lee: prostitution network boss
Andrew Russman: suspected bank robber and associate of
 Richard Henkel
Sasha Scott: prostitute
Laurence Windsor: suspected bank robber and associate of
 Richard Henkel

CHAPTER 1

It was the day before Christmas Eve, 1977, and downtown Pittsburgh was stirring. As the end of the workday approached, Golden Triangle office employees donned Santa hats and threw parties. Workers clocked out early to meet friends, wrap gifts, or prepare for family gatherings. Shoppers dashed in and out of little shops or the multilevels like Joseph Horne and Gimbels.

On the second floor of 641 Liberty Avenue, above the Slack Shop boutique and an adult movie theater, the Gemini Spa was open for business. The Gemini was an upscale version of the "rub-and-tug joints." They became popular in the 1960s with the rapid rise in the commercialization of the sex trade. There had long been cheap hookers on street corners. Now, higher-class "escorts" could easily be found at downtown lounges. Adult "literature" and novelty shops, strip joints, and massage parlors were popping up on lower Penn and Liberty Avenues.

The Gemini's waiting area held a few chairs and a registration desk. A stack of blank forms was ready for recording times, payments, and services rendered—pleasure and relief, of course, maybe even a massage. Despite an unhallowed blend of yule and prostitution, the ladies of Gemini had decorated a Christmas tree. It featured joyfully in front of the white-curtained windows.

The line of shotgun shells on the windowsill did not. A message for clients?

Several Gemini "goddesses" chatted with holiday season excitement and anticipation while eagerly awaiting a client to walk through the door. Among the youngest and prettiest of these twenty-somethings was raven-haired Sasha Scott. Her start in the flesh racket came on the heels of a troubling childhood. By age sixteen, she had left her Milwaukee suburb, fell in love with a much older pimp named Glenn Scott, settled in Pittsburgh, and married him in 1975. Three months later, they separated. He had proven to be an abusive and violent partner. Six months later, someone proved to be even more violent with Scotty. And then he was dead.

But that was two years earlier. Now Sasha was over her grief, back to work, and more in demand than ever. She mingled with the other Gemini girls around the Christmas pine and the few presents below, gifted from appreciative and lonely clients. Sasha received the most gifts. Mainly trinkets. Sasha had already received one present from one of her favorite and wealthiest clients. And it was a biggie—the talk of the spa.

When the door opened, the girls expected to see a client. But it was a taxi driver who had been paid to deliver a Christmas present. Another one for Sasha.

* * *

The land called Pittsburgh rises from the convergence of three rivers, the Ohio, the Monongahela, and the Allegheny, to the foothills of the Allegheny Mountains. "The city lies unevenly upon unruly land," wrote author Martin Aurand in his book *The Spectator and the Topographical City*. "Communities and neighborhoods are variously defined by hills and demarcated by hollows. Buildings may be two stories on one side and four or five on another. There are a great number and variety of contrivances for scaling, connecting, and otherwise negotiating the terrain, ranging from bridges to tunnels to inclined plains and public steps."

The Henkels lived on Upland Street at the crest of a hill in Homewood. A steep stairwell led to the modest bungalow with a brick front porch. This residential section of Pittsburgh's far east side was once the landing zone for German, Irish, and Italian immigrants.

Frank Henkel, a German American, eventually worked his way up from an office clerk to yardman for the Pennsylvania Railroad. The avid bowler and his wife, Hannah, had a daughter and three sons. On a spring afternoon in 1941, Richard, the youngest child at the time, slipped outside. The toddler walked down to the street and made his way into the family car. While climbing around, Richard released the parking brake. The car started rolling backward, and the runaway vehicle quickly accelerated with its captive lad. It careened down the street for two houses, ran off the roadway, then slammed into a parked car—sending it smashing through a brick pillar of the porch on another house. The boy was jolted but uninjured. Hours later, Richard was still sullen-faced when his parents permitted him to pose for a news photographer next to the neighbor's damaged car. Little Richard Henkel was only three years old. But he had already generated newspaper coverage in his first instance of mayhem.

In 1945, Frank and Hannah had a fourth son they would name Robert. By all accounts, the Henkels were a middle-class, loving, and church-going Baptist family.

"We did not lack for any necessities," Richard would later say. "Dad and Mom took us on family vacations, to family reunions, and to amusement parks. They took us fishing often."

5

Little else is known about Richard's childhood. He dropped out of high school halfway through ninth grade.

"I was not failing," Henkel later wrote. "I was a solid student but never took a book home. My parents were upset and wanted me to go back to school."

Instead, Richard took a job at an Isaly's store. The popular deli and ice cream parlor chain featured their Klondikes, thick vanilla ice cream slices covered in chocolate, and their "Skyscraper," a famous mile-high scoop of ice cream in a cone, one of which came free with each purchase.

"I was a master at making Skyscraper cones," Henkel recalled laughingly.

As a head clerk, Richard, age sixteen, was responsible for opening and closing the store twice weekly. His ice cream career did not last long.

"I got fired because I had sex with a pretty twenty-two-year-old customer. The next day, me and my buddy, the assistant manager, were downstairs changing into our whites. Like an idiot, I told him I had sex in the store. He went right upstairs and told the manager. I got fired, walked out, caught a street car and went home."

At age seventeen, Richard joined the US Air Force and committed to four years of service and an additional two years of reserve status. He was sent to Sampson Air Force Base in New York. After basic training, he completed six months of technical school and was certified as a propeller mechanic to work on C-119 and C-130 transport planes in Smyrna, Tennessee. He also obtained his GED high school equivalency certification and seemed pleased with the accomplishment.

"I took the GED without any prep. I just took it and passed."

Later, Richard was stationed in Munich and Frankfurt, where he studied the German language using tapes he had purchased.

During his military service, he was awarded a Good Conduct Medal for conducting himself with professionalism and discipline, consistently earning excellent assessment ratings, and perfect attendance at service schools.

In 1958, after his four-year commitment, Richard was honorably discharged and transferred to reserve status. The good conduct medal he had earned belied what would happen after he returned to Pittsburgh.

For two years, Richard worked various jobs. He opened a dairy story with his oldest brother. "It was called 'Henkel's Dairy,'" Richard recalled. "It was in a bad location, and we went out of business."

Richard worked at the Westinghouse Electrical Corporation and also as a union laborer. But in 1960, when he was twenty-three, he veered off course. Richard and an accomplice robbed a Pittsburgh gas station and, after striking the attendant in the head with a wrench, they fled in a Fiat. Police officers spotted their car and gave chase. The thieves threw some of their stolen bills out the window and eluded the first officers. After being apprehended by Penn Hills cops, both young men were convicted and given prison sentences of eighteen months.

Nineteen sixty-three was a tough year for the Henkel family. Richard was released from prison, but his father, Frank Henkel, suffered a massive heart attack at his railroad office and died. He was fifty-eight. A month later, Richard's older brother, George, a US Navy veteran, was killed in an automobile crash.

"George was a good brother," Richard said. "It was painful for me when he left this earth."

After the loss of his brother and father, Richard continued to rack up criminal charges.

As the 1965 holiday season approached, Richard, now twenty-eight, was arrested for his involvement in a burglary ring.

One of their targets was a food warehouse. Police searched his girlfriend's house and located twelve hundred dollars' worth of stolen cigarettes.

As Pittsburghers welcomed 1966, cops were on the lookout for a 1959 blue sedan wanted in connection with purchases made with a stolen credit card. It was among ten lifted from the Pittsburgh Athletic Association's locker room. When patrol officers spotted the car, Richard Henkel was behind the wheel. He was in the company of two young women. The vehicle was registered to a US Steel Corporation executive. Henkel had managed to intercept the man's mail at his hotel a few weeks earlier. In an early version of identity theft, Henkel used his victim's personal information to obtain license plates. He was arrested and charged with larceny, forgery, and auto theft.

Before his case was adjudicated, Henkel tried his luck outside the city. He and an accomplice headed north to Erie, Pennsylvania. They found a grocery store that was positioned well for a break-in. After breaching the building, they headed for the office. They successfully defeated the safe and pulled out $1,400 in cash. As they made their escape, two Pittsburgh State Police officers nabbed them inside the building.

Little is known about the disposition of Richard Henkel's previous arrests, but during this time, he still managed to find someone who would take his hand in marriage. But neither his wife, Carol, nor the subsequent birth of their one child altered Richard's life path.

CHAPTER 2

Richard Henkel capped the 1960s with a spate of bank jobs. In January 1969, he broke into two banks while they were closed. When he burglarized downtown's Fort Pitt Savings and Loan branch, he escaped with $12,000 in American Express travelers checks. The next day, Henkel and accomplice James M. Barone broke into the First State Savings and Loan Association in McCandless Township. Again, they walked with travelers checks, savings bonds, blank money orders, and $6,000 cash. In April, FBI agents arrested Henkel for the second heist.

When FBI agents obtained an arrest warrant for the First State Savings burglary, Henkel was free on a $5,000 bond. They spotted him driving and attempted to halt his car, but Henkel stepped on the gas and headed into the Squirrel Hill neighborhood. He stopped abruptly and bailed out. Henkel sprinted for nearly a mile before the agents and Pittsburgh cops caught him. The next day, Barone was arrested in Youngstown, Ohio.

Despite being placed under an additional $5,000 bond, Henkel produced bail. He laid low for a couple of months, then he went back to work. On a July morning, tellers at the Keystone Bank in Duquesne, a tiny burg southeast of the city and on the Monongahela River, were preparing to open. They were loading their drawers with cash from the vault when Henkel and an accomplice, brandishing pistols, emerged from a back room. They wore ski masks and black gloves. While holding the employees at gunpoint, the robbers emptied cash from the drawers into their large briefcase. They then grabbed more money from the vault. Finally, one of them ordered the manager to give up his keys. A newspaper reporter would later write that, before fleeing in his car, Henkel and left his victims coffee and doughnuts.

While the bank employees waited for police and FBI agents to arrive, the two robbers raced out and jumped into a preplaced car. Just two miles from the bank, they pulled in front of some businesses and screeched to a stop. They jumped out, scrambled into a second car, and continued their getaway.

When FBI agents arrived at the bank, they found no forced entry to the building. Baffled, they eventually determined that the burglars had slipped into the bank during the hour before opening, when the employees arrived at work. And when they departed, they had left with $80,000—the largest amount of cash stolen in all of Pittsburgh's twenty-one bank robberies in 1969.

Two days after the Keystone Bank heist, employees of the Mars National Bank branch, just north of the city, became suspicious of a customer. He was white, about thirty years old, had a full head of dark hair, and carried a large black briefcase. He identified himself as Richard Edward and rented a safe-deposit box. After he left, the manager checked his listed address and found no such number and street combination. He notified the FBI. It was a time before bank surveillance cameras recorded continuously. The FBI agent instructed the manager to take a photo of the man if he returned.

A few weeks later, the man came back in. The manager activated the surveillance camera and snapped his photograph. Later, FBI agents identified the culprit as Richard Henkel.

In the Keystone Bank robbery, agents identified Henkel's accomplice as Laurence Paul Windsor, a resident of Pittsburgh's Squirrel Hill neighborhood. He hailed from England and was brought to the US as a child. Federal bank robbery warrants were issued for both men. Henkel remained a fugitive. FBI agents and Pittsburgh cops had him high on their list of wanted persons. As the months passed and the weather got cold, their search warmed.

Agents tracked Henkel to a hotel southeast of the city near Kennywood Amusement Park and arrested him. He was registered under the alias of Richard Sayman. Andrew Russman, one of Henkel's fellow thieves, was there using the name of Andy Hendricks. Russman, from the Allentown community on Pittsburgh's South Side, was arrested for violating his bond from another case.

Laurence Windsor and James Barone, Henkel's associate from Youngstown, Ohio, remained at large. Russman was charged with, and pleaded guilty to, harboring a fugitive. Then, like Barone, he dropped off law enforcement radar.

Once FBI agents identified Henkel from the bank surveillance video, they obtained a search warrant for the safe-deposit box at the Mars National Bank branch. Inside they found $20,000. They traced the cash to the Keystone Bank. Henkel was held in jail in lieu of a $150,000 bond. When investigators prepared to have tellers identify Henkel from a lineup, he refused to wear his toupee. At five feet eleven inches, slim, with dark hair and a bushy unibrow, Henkel possessed a rather benign appearance. A disarming smile veiled his criminal tendencies. Richard had not escaped the rapid progression of male pattern baldness through his twenties. By age thirty, generous hair on the sides of his head remained to flank a bald dome. Henkel took to wearing toupees. He may not have been vain.

* * *

To Richard E. Henkel: Participate in the lineup and wear your toupee!

A federal judge issued this command in response to a petition filed by the assistant US attorney who was handling Henkel's bank robbery charge. Henkel donned and doffed hairpieces as a tactic to stymie witnesses. Reluctantly, he patted down his wig and stood for the lineup. The Keystone Bank employees promptly identified him as one of the men who robbed them at gunpoint.

Meanwhile, Henkel went to trial for the January 18 Fort Pitt Savings and Loan burglary. Two of his associates claimed he confessed to hitting the bank. But Henkel's defense attorney, David O'Hanesian, cited discrepancies in the details of their statements. As a result, he won Henkel an acquittal.

In the meantime, Carol Henkel had enough of her criminally inclined husband. But the divorce was actually amicable, with Henkel's primary concern being visitation privileges with his one-year-old son.

"It was apparent to me that he had a great deal of love for his son," said Mrs. Henkel's attorney.

In an ironic twist, Carol went on to work as a clerk for the Allegheny County police academy.

In the Allegheny County Jail, Henkel awaited trial for the Keystone Bank robbery. One of his fellow inmates was Peter J. Biagiarelli, an old friend awaiting trial with two others for robbing and killing a former Marine who was disabled. Somehow, Henkel convinced Biagiarelli to own the Keystone Bank rap. He agreed. Henkel's defense attorney presented the accused killer as a surprise witness. Biagiarelli testified that he robbed Keystone Bank then gave Henkel $20,000 to hold and told him he won it gambling. He said he and fugitive Laurence Windsor pulled off the heist together. Henkel maintained his innocence. He offered that his only mistake was running from authorities.

After conducting separate interviews, US Attorney Blair A. Griffith suspected that Henkel coached Biagiarelli about details of the bank robbery and set him up to take the blame. To confirm his theory, Griffith conducted a courtroom lineup. He instructed the bank teller victims, and other random persons, to stand up for Biagiarelli to identify. When he could not identify who was an employee and who was not, the ruse ended. Henkel was convicted. In September 1970, the judge sentenced him to twenty years. Meanwhile, FBI agents continued to search for Windsor.

Shortly after Henkel entered the US Penitentiary at Marion, Illinois, a federal grand jury indicted him for a charge in a case involving $1 million dollars in counterfeit postage stamps. He was convicted and sentenced to serve time concurrently with his twenty-year bank robbery sentence.

CHAPTER 3

While Richard Henkel was in Marion Penitentiary, he often expressed concern for his son. Some administrators found him to be intelligent and polite. He participated in various educational courses. He joined the prison's historical society and the Jaycees (United States Junior Chamber of Commerce), a civic organization that provided training in business skills and leadership.

Meanwhile, in Pittsburgh's underworld, ongoing dramatic events would soon factor into Henkel's future. It all started with a local ironworker named George E. Lee. During the daytime, Lee wore a gray work shirt and steel-toe boots and drove a rusty pickup. When the sun fell, he maintained his attire but switched to his red Cadillac convertible with white leather upholstery. When he left his fashionable South Hills apartment, the destination was always the Golden Triangle. Sometimes, a sexy employee accompanied him to his headquarters at Studio One, a massage parlor (and more) on Ninth Street. When the demand for commercialized sex increased in the 1960s, investors like Lee took an interest in the supply side.

Despite several arrests and a 1973 conviction for keeping a "bawdy house," Lee was Pittsburgh's top dog in the flourishing porn and pay-for-sex rackets. As an adult, he learned the ironworker trade. Between the 1940s and 1960s, he traveled the country at a time when the steel industry was red-hot and construction projects were booming. He settled in Texas and got married. One day, George returned home unexpectedly.

"I found my very best friend with my first wife," he said. "I just had to shoot him. If he was a perfect stranger, then I'd a had to shoot my wife dead."

After serving five years for the attempted murder rap, Lee returned to ironworking. He served as a crew foreman for the renovation of the grand Heinz Hall for the Performing Arts. Then he grew bored with his spare time.

"I started my business as a sideline," he said. "I was just tired of watching television at night."

Within a few years, George Lee amassed a small empire of entertainment clubs, sex theaters, go-go bars, and massage parlors. They included the Rabbit Patch, Taurean, Aardvark, and Maya. Because of his criminal record, Lee's businesses, especially those requiring liquor licenses, were owned on paper by trusted straw purchasers. Most were under an umbrella corporation, which Lee named *Bella*, meaning beautiful in many Latin tongues. Lee was also associated with Majestic News, a distributor of films and magazines featuring explicit sex. It was part of the far-flung naughty empire of Cleveland-based smut baron Reuben Sturman.

Lee ran his businesses in a rather loosely controlled federation overseen by lieutenants Dante "Tex" Gill, Nick Delucia, and Mel Cummings. Gill was born a woman but identified as a man. Delucia was a former city fireman linked by family ties to a prominent member of the Pittsburgh crime family run by John LaRocca. Cummings was an Army veteran with an interstate gambling conviction.

Then, of course, there were the service providers—the young women. And in some cases, young men. With the right connections, the better-looking and better-skilled might wind up as higher-paid call girls or so-called escorts. They were in their late teens to early thirties, had varied backgrounds, but shared key traits.

"If you check the background of all these girls, you'll find they came from many different jobs," said Pittsburgh Police Superintendent Robert Coll. "But most relate to bars and to nightlife when they get to meet people of that caliber."

Many of these prostitutes started on the streets then opted for the relatively better working conditions of massage parlors, such as the Gemini Spa, one of George Lee's featured venues. Tempting newspaper advertisements beckoned clients.

World-renowned soothing body rubs by lovely female attendants. If you enjoy the finer things in life, then we're what you've been looking for. Let us introduce you to Brandy, Francine, and Sasha.

CHAPTER 4

By the mid-twentieth century, two dozen US major cities, including Pittsburgh, were home to so-called Mafia families, each comprised primarily of Italian American criminals and headed by a boss, sometimes referred to as a godfather. This network of mostly autonomous organized crime groups, also known as *La Cosa Nostra* (meaning "Our Thing" in Italian), was loosely overseen by the Mafia ruling commission, which was comprised of five Mafia families in New York City. La Cosa Nostra was allied with powerful mobsters—many of whom were Jewish—and corrupt government officials and labor union officers. But the alliance included racketeers of every ethnicity and tendency—bookmakers and other gambling operators, forgers, extortionists, gambling operators, hustlers, thieves, stickup men, killers, their wannabe associates, and their misguided molls, young women delighted with gang life. The more skill and income an individual brought to the organization, the more he was valued by the bosses.

When Prohibition ended the mob's cash cow, gambling became a mainstay cash machine for every crime family across the US. Many citizens considered it a victimless crime, as they did sex-for-pay. In many cities, "the numbers," or illegal lottery, harked back to the 1920s and gained popularity through the next several decades. By the 1960s, Pittsburgh's Tony Grosso headed one of the biggest numbers games in the country. State legislators, seeing the potential for ongoing infusions to coffers, created lottery commissions. In 1972, the Pennsylvania Lottery Commission launched its first game. As the legal games became more popular, they siphoned gambling dollars from organized crime. Some experts believe the mob, to make up for the losses, moved in on the rub parlor racket in some cities.

"After all," one police source said, "[massage parlor prostitution] is one of the few organized crime rackets that can be advertised in the newspaper."

State and local lawmen investigating the massage parlor racket uncovered specific connections to the Pittsburgh mob. They said rub parlor lieutenant Nick Delucia was linked, through marriage, to Joseph "Jo Jo" Pecora, a high-ranking Pittsburgh Mafia member who operated out of Chester, West Virginia.

With the opening of additional mob-connected and independent parlors selling sex, "massage" became a dirty word. And Raymond Sledge was out to halt the spreading perception. Sledge—a black businessman—was a professional masseuse, owned a massage school, and was vice president of the Pennsylvania Massage Association. So naturally, he touted the therapeutic benefits of hands-on kneading of muscles and soft tissue. He was also a longtime leader in the efforts to regulate the massage business and stamp out parlors whose stock-in-trade was sex.

In the 1960s and 1970s, law enforcement agencies often made little progress in their prostitution cases. Some politicians struggled privately, if not publicly, with the idea of legislating morals. It was an era when many states rewrote laws that had gone unenforced. Those laws criminalized conduct such as living "in a state of adultery and fornication" without being married.

Ethically challenged and greedy officials accepted bribes in exchange for looking the other way. And investigators faced strategic and ethical challenges gathering evidence. Their few successful cases often resulted in relatively minor charges and penalties.

When Sledge pushed for state regulation of massage parlors, one promising bill passed the Pennsylvania House and Senate. But Governor Milton J. Shapp vetoed it because he found the bill "objectionable from the standpoint of consumer protection, administrative feasibility, and constitutionality." One of his representatives said his position was that prostitution laws should be enforced at the local level. After Shapp vetoed that bill, more massage parlors opened in Pittsburgh's lower Liberty and Penn Avenue neighborhood, the city's red light district. According to police sources, the customers were getting more than rubdowns.

A *Pittsburgh Press* editorial weighed in:

"Some enforcement controls over massage parlors are needed to outlaw those that are nothing but sex shops in disguise and to halt the proliferation of seedy enterprises that threaten the main business districts of every large city in the state."

"They are ruining the reputation of our profession," said Raymond Sledge.

In response to the problem, Mayor Pete Flaherty's administration proposed legislation banning intersexual massages. Several business organizations offered their support. Police Superintendent Robert Coll did, too, but felt it would not solve other problems, such as citizens being harassed as they walked through the red light district.

Two Pittsburgh City Council members, Eugene P. DePasquale and Amy Ballinger, wanted to see firsthand if the new legislation was needed. So, with news reporters and a photographer tagging along, they visited a Liberty Avenue massage parlor. An attendant assured them the operation was "good for the city and nothing more than an extension of growing leisure field in the US." She said the operation was legal and that it was patronized by very nice, lonely gentlemen.

DePasquale asked if he could have a sample massage. "Goddess Minerva" had him remove his shirt. Then she gave him a brief rubdown while the reporters looked on.

Afterward, he said, "I can't really see anything illegitimate about it."

Ballinger concurred, though the councilwoman objected to an adjacent business screening adult-oriented films.

The following day, the *Pittsburgh Post-Gazette* titled their story of the visit, "DePasquale is Rubbed the Right Way."

Post-Gazette staff writer Robert Voelker conducted his own investigation. He ventured into the Roman V and found the place carpeted, well-furnished, and clean.

"It obviously represented a hefty investment for someone," he wrote.

When choosing from several young women waiting to serve, the reporter selected Suzy. She led him to a small room and told him to lay face down on the massage table. He plunked down twenty bucks for a full-body rubdown and another ten dollars for her to work topless. They made small talk while Suzy worked his muscles. She said she was twenty-two and got the job after answering an advertisement. She told him to flip over on his back.

"The same top-to-bottom pattern was followed," he later wrote. "With that, it was time for the main event. Suzy said, 'We also offer hand relief.' Naturally, I declined the offer, knowing it would be naughty."

Voelker also visited the Maya Spa in downtown Market Square. He described it as "seedy" but said the services and procedures were essentially the same as Roman V.

Meanwhile, Allen Brunwasser defended five of the city's massage parlor owners who challenged the ban on female-to-male rubdowns. The lawyer raised eyebrows when he suggested to Pittsburgh City Council members that the rub joints were good for convention business. His description of the rub girls as "cultured ladies of considerable intellect" sparked muffled laughs.

"The only thing going on in those places is massaging," Brunwasser said.

"Do you consider a legitimate massage a good time?" a councilman asked.

"Well, yes . . . but of course, there is a different feeling when a girl massages a guy."

"I guess it's the lighter touch," another councilman said, prompting more laughter.

PART 2

Lead Characters:

Richard Henkel

Bruce Agnew: burglar and associate of Kripplebauer and Henkel

Joseph "Joey D" DeMarco: Mafia associate and operator of the
    Court Lounge

Suzanne Dixon: Henkel's girlfriend and close friend of Sasha Scott

Allan Frendzel: small-time criminal; associate of Richard Henkel

Debbie Gentile: employee of Richard Henkel

Robert Henkel: brother to Richard

Louis Kripplebauer: notorious burglar and associate of Richard
    Henkel

Mike Lackovic: Allegheny County Police homicide detective

Robert Payne: Allegheny County Police homicide detective

Glenn "Scotty" Scott: small-time criminal and pimp

Joann "Sasha" Scott: prostitute and close friend of Suzanne
    Dixon

Gary Small: police officer and friend of Richard Henkel

CHAPTER 5

In 1972, while at Marion federal prison in Illinois, Richard Henkel befriended fellow inmate Roy Travis, a thirty-one-year-old Canadian pilot in his fifth year of a seventeen-year sentence for drug smuggling. A Royal Canadian Mounted Police member previously described him as a bright young man who attended the University of British Columbia and served with the Royal Canadian Air Force. Travis was also an electronics whiz. In later years, his expertise would attract Henkel's attention. In the meantime, the two inmates spent some of their time at a chessboard.

"Roy was a good chess player," Richard recalled. "Better than me."

Henkel's prison time during the early 1970s coincided with the final years of the Vietnam War, the legalization of abortion in the US, and the resignation of President Richard Nixon. During this period, Henkel was progressing well in a two-year John A. Logan College program in psychology. His interest in the subject came from a "wonderful professor who made the material come alive." Henkel consistently impressed officials with his behavior and a 4.7 grade point average. His first shot at parole occurred in 1974 after serving only four years. If there was a god of criminal sentences, he must have been smiling down on the convicted bank robber. A prison assessment described Richard as a "psychologically stable person interested in making a positive contribution to society." So federal parole authorities cut him loose.

Richard L. Thornburg, US attorney for the Western District of Pennsylvania, took exception. "I'm not trying to assign blame, but something's wrong when men sentenced to twenty years for violent crimes are out in a matter of months."

In late 1974, Henkel was paroled to Youngstown, Ohio, the home of his mother and his brother Robert, who worked for US Steel Corporation. Richard took a job in a foreign car repair shop.

Youngstown, just over an hour's drive from Pittsburgh, is set along a stretch of Ohio's Mahoning River. As with Cleveland and Pittsburgh, the area thrived as part of America's so-called rust belt of steel manufacturing. But in the 1960s and 1970s, the economy tanked due to a combination of factors, including the pressure of foreign competition, automation of machines, and steel plant closings. The Mafia, with ready supplies of cash and protection from dishonest government officials of every stripe, had a firm grip on the cities of Youngstown, Warren, and the rest of the Mahoning Valley. The numbers racket and sports gambling—diversions of fun and hope for the struggling blue-collar population—brought in fast cash. Vending machines carrying candy and cigarettes, and pinball machines, generated piles of coins. Vending routes could be muscled from competitors. And they were easy targets for "skimming," a common method of stealing from business receipts and, in turn, reducing taxable income totals.

The men who called the shots in this network had colorful nicknames. Jasper "Fats" Aiello, James "Blackie" Licavoli, Donald "Moosey" Caputo, and Tony "Dope" Delsanter had ties to the mighty Cleveland and Pittsburgh Mafia families.

From the early 1950s to the early 1960s, periodic battles broke out in the Mahoning County underworld. According to the FBI, part of the conflict began when mob lieutenant Frank Brancato forced a Youngstown vending machine operator to cut the Cleveland family in for one-third of his profits. To ensure continued cash flow, Brancato had his enforcers bring the man new customers. When his competitors became resentful, shootings and bombings followed. There were so many explosions that the Mahoning Valley was dubbed "Crimetown, USA" and "Bombtown, USA." Car bombings became known as "Youngstown tune-ups."

The Youngstown tune-up performed on the most recent Cadillac purchased by Charlie Cavallaro (known as Charlie Cadillac) was a tragic example of a critical flaw of bombings: innocent victims. A well-known racketeer who was at war over control of Youngstown gambling interests, Cavallaro was getting into his car with his two sons when a bomb detonated. He was killed, as intended. But the bungled job also resulted in the death of his eleven-year-old boy. The other son, twelve, survived but suffered debilitating injuries.

The murder and maiming of the Cavallaro boys drew the ire of the police, the media, and those citizens who had otherwise tolerated the mob as a sort of regional subculture. The two Mafia factions knew they had to make changes. They called a truce and then agreed on territorial boundaries. Youngstown and most of Mahoning County would be Pittsburgh territory under the supervision of Jimmy Prato. Two neighboring counties, and part of Mahoning County, would go to the Cleveland mob as overseen by Tony Delsanter. When Delsanter died, the job went to Ronald Carabbia, one of three brothers well-established within the Cleveland and Youngstown network of Mafia associates and mobbed-up burglars.

* * *

A few months after his release, in September 1975, Richard moved from Youngstown to Pittsburgh where he looked forward to visits with his son, now seven years old. Henkel rented a room then ran into Gary Small, a childhood friend of his brother Robert. Now Small was a decorated combat veteran of the US Marines. After his service in the Vietnam War, he joined the police force. The athletic, good-looking, blue-eyed cop had taken his oath to protect and serve in Edgewood Borough on the city's eastern border three years earlier. He was described as a quiet but respected cop. In his spare time, Small participated in a sportsmen's club. Eventually, the members elected him as an officer with partial control over ownership of the association's land.

Small, recently separated from his wife, suggested to Henkel that they share an apartment. Henkel agreed.

"Gary was a good cop and was respected by his fellow officers, his chief, and Edgewood business owners. I knew he served in Vietnam, but he never talked about it. He was not a bragger. I trusted Gary even more than my friend, Henry Ford. I could tell Gary anything, but we did not socialize like me and Henry. I trusted Henry but did not ever tell him about things he did not need to know."

Henkel and Small lived together for only two months before Richard found his own place. In the weeks following that period, Gary Small's wife made a police report with a shocking allegation. It would lay buried for five years. Meanwhile, Richard moved out of the apartment with Small and rented a unit in the Chatham Crane Apartments off Crane Avenue in the west side neighborhood of Banksville, near the Liberty Tunnel. Based on past relationships from his bank robbery days, and new connections he made in prison, Richard established himself in Pittsburgh's underworld of hookers, massage parlor workers, drug dealers, prostitutes, burglars, mobbed-up associates, and contract killers. To them, he was known as "Dick."

Henkel hooked up with James Louis Kripplebauer Jr., a leader in the K&A Gang of notorious burglars from Cherry Hill, New Jersey. Called "Junior" by his friends, Kripplebauer and his crack team had been wreaking havoc with stealthy thefts from the homes of wealthy residents across several states. Pittsburgh became a stopover.

As burglars faced improved alarm system technology, many moved to the fast and fat profits of selling narcotics. Kripplebauer's network of burglars and dope peddlers included Philadelphia hoodlums Bruce Agnew and Jack Siggson.

Siggson served time for shooting and killing a man during a fight in Camden County, New Jersey. Henkel first met him when he picked him up at Pittsburgh International Airport after Siggson couriered two ounces of heroin for Kripplebauer. He looked five years older than Henkel but was several years younger. He was sharp-nosed, sported a beard, and wore tinted eyeglasses. Richard and the others in his circle referred to Siggson as "Jack the Jew."

* * *

By 1976, Richard, now thirty-eight, shared his apartment with his live-in girlfriend, Suzanne Dixon, thirty-one. A blonde, blue-eyed product of a large Irish Catholic family, Suzanne was slender, attractive and a sharp dresser. Overly generous, she would pick up dinner or bar tabs for her girlfriends or provide cash to friends in need.

"And Suzanne was a sucker for hurt and endangered animals," Henkel said. "She donated money to save elephants, whales, and big cats. I think she was on every sucker list. Suzanne was funny and adorable with a heart as big as the sky and was the only person I trusted to watch my son who was eight years old."

Henkel recalled a time when he gave Suzanne two rings, one with a five-carat diamond and one with a two-carat diamond.

"The rings were too small, so I told her to see my jeweler in the Clark Building to put the diamonds in new settings. I told her not to leave the stones there. She did and I got upset and explained how easy it would be to replace them with lesser-quality diamonds. Suzanne said, 'He's your jeweler, he would not cheat you. And he's got an honest face.' She was too trusting."

Suzanne was part of a loose and murky network of underworld dwellers and their groupies—bar employees, hookers, pimps, burglars, stickup men, low-level wise guys, and even killers connected to Pittsburgh's prostitution, gambling, and drug rackets. Many of them drank and worked deals at the Court Lounge. Various temptresses mingled throughout the day, on display for by-the-hour companionship. As a result, clients and others referred to the Court Lounge as the "bus stop."

The popular lounge and restaurant was named for its location across from the downtown Allegheny County criminal courts building. The lounge's owner was said to be Antonio Ripepi, a senior member of the Pittsburgh Mafia, but Joseph "Joey D" DeMarco, a mob associate, had run the place since 1965.

DeMarco supplemented his income with gambling operations and narcotics sales. When problems arose, he had several thugs, including six-foot three-inch, 210-pound Charles "Chuckie" Kellington, on his payroll. Kellington was a ninth-grade dropout. He served in the US Army, was honorably discharged, and then went to work in a steel mill. He claimed that repeated layoffs led him to the Court Lounge as bartender. Then, he went to work as an enforcer for DeMarco's drug and gambling operations.

Among others in DeMarco's network were Youngstown mob soldier Joe DeRose Jr. and Richard Henkel.

CHAPTER 6

Nineteen-year-old Joann Scott was one of Joey DeMarco's favorite dolls of the evening. She was adored by many at the Court Lounge. Men and women. And not just those who paid.

Joann and her friend Suzanne Dixon had met while working at the Court Lounge—Joann as a popular prostitute and Suzanne as assistant manager of the nightclub and restaurant.

Joann was seventeen when she met Glenn "Scotty" Scott in 1973. The black pimp, burglar, and dope dealer hailed from the tiny borough of Houston, Pennsylvania, a thirty-minute drive south of Pittsburgh. He was thirty-eight years old and smitten with the teenager's beauty. "You look like a Russian princess," he told Joann.

Glenn started calling her Sasha. And the nickname stuck. Glenn got a job as a doorman and elevator operator at the Edison Hotel. The downscale location at Penn Avenue and Ninth Street featured a burlesque stage with striptease acts like Dynamite Dottie, Sheena the Fantastic Savage, and Torsha the Champagne Lady of Burlesque—who also worked as a prostitute in the Nick Delucia network. Glenn found the Edison to be a productive location for Sasha. Soon, he moved them to an apartment in Pittsburgh's Oakland neighborhood, an increasingly vibrant area of museums, universities, and hospitals.

Then Manpower money became available. The Allegheny County program, subsidized with federal taxpayer dollars, provided unemployed persons with job training and also sponsored summer programs for children. Glenn, using the influence of politically connected contacts, was awarded $30,000. He used it to lease property from the Richland County Youth Foundation, a half-hour drive north of Pittsburgh. The deal included a farmhouse, stables, a run-down barn, and a riding ring. Glenn renovated it into a day camp and riding academy for disadvantaged children. He named it S&S—presumably Scotty and Sasha. He also boarded horses and provided others for riding.

It appeared that Glenn Scott might be turning his life around and on his way to a happy life with his youthful princess. He and Sasha moved into the S&S farmhouse. Glenn established the summer programs, and the camp became a hangout for his pal, Steelers fullback Franco Harris, and several of his teammates who volunteered with children throughout Pittsburgh. Glenn Scott's soft spot for needy kids, however, was dubious.

Meanwhile, Sasha's willingness and knack for attracting eager and well-paying clients had served its purpose. Now, Glenn wanted her off the market, away from the recreational drugs that permeated her lifestyle, and all to himself. She agreed with the plan, and in the summer of 1974, they married. It was a grand wedding at Pittsburgh's ornate Saint Paul Cathedral, an architectural gem in the Gothic Revival style. Franco Harris served as Scotty's best man.

If there was any wedded bliss for Glenn and Sasha Scott, it didn't last long. Eighteen-year-old Sasha's unbridled ambitions were no match for her forty-year-old husband's swerve away from the nightlife in which they met. Conflict soon entered the newly minted marriage. Glenn was uncompromising and physically abusive. During one assault, he broke his bride's nose.

"When [Mafia associate and Court Lounge boss] Joey DeMarco saw her, he was furious with Glenn," a bar regular recalled. "Joey wasn't happy about the mixed marriage in the first place."

Three months after they married, Sasha and Glenn separated. She moved in with Suzanne and Richard. As the months rolled on, Henkel became annoyed with her presence. Sasha was Suzanne's very close friend, but to Richard, she was a stranger who could overhear his telephone conversations and see his visitors. Suzanne refused to ask her to leave.

Meanwhile, Sasha returned to the relationships she knew best—no-strings-attached sex-for-cash. She resumed working out of the Court Lounge, much to the approval of Joey D. On one occasion, Glenn Scott showed up in the parking lot and tried to beckon her away. DeMarco sent two thugs to greet him, and Scotty went home bleeding. But Glenn soon had other problems bigger than persona non grata status at the Court Lounge. A scandal emerged with Manpower as program recipients sucked up the federal grant funding without delivering full value. Some, like Glenn Scott, were allegedly paying ghost employees and billing excessively for purchases that failed to reach the intended child beneficiaries. Manpower fraud throughout Allegheny County eventually amounted to several million in taxpayer dollars.

His estrangement from Sasha, and the stress of the Manpower fraud investigation, weighed on Glenn Scott. He became increasingly desperate and reached out for friends to help him win back his wife. Like many young women in her orbit, Sasha was a poor judge of character, especially at the intersection of men and love. She was convinced that Glenn's intentions were noble and moved back. Their reconciliation was brief and tumultuous. After Glenn forced Sasha's head into a toilet, she left and moved back with Richard Henkel and Suzanne Dixon. Two days later, Sasha was at the Court Lounge when Scotty telephoned and threatened her. She was fearful and upset, so Suzanne called Richard and asked him to drive her home. When Richard arrived, Sasha got in his car, and they drove to the apartment. Neither was aware that Glenn was sitting in his car nearby, lying in wait.

Henkel pulled up the hilly entrance drive into Chatham Crane. As Sasha stepped out, Glenn intercepted.

He grabbed her arm and said to Richard, "This is my wife."

"Wait a minute," Henkel said while exiting his car. "She doesn't want to go with you."

"She's my wife. And she's nineteen."

"I don't care how old she is," Henkel said. "She said she doesn't want to go with you. She's not going."

Glenn stepped over to his car and reached in. He pulled out a pistol and aimed it at Henkel. "Now get back in your car."

Henkel backed off. While Scotty's attention was on him reentering his car, Sasha bolted. She ran down a grass embankment. Glenn pursued her. When both were out of view, Henkel heard a shot.

CHAPTER 7

Before she was Sasha Scott, she was Joann Maniscalco. The pretty girl with jet-black hair hailed from Whitefish Bay, Wisconsin, a Milwaukee suburb perched above Lake Michigan. She was the middle child of three kids.

Joann's childhood spanned the 1960s with racial turbulence and riots, a cultural shift toward sexual freedom, and mantra of "question authority." Her own social problems began during her final weeks of sixth grade at a Catholic school. Her male lay teacher, a rookie educator and harsh disciplinarian, summoned Joann's parents for a conference. He told them she had not been participating and he had decided to hold her back from attending seventh grade.

"The teacher only lasted one year," recalled a close family member. "I felt like the Catholic school had hired someone who couldn't cut it in the better-respected local public system. Why didn't he notify her parents of the problem earlier?"

Having to repeat sixth grade was a blow to Joann's ego. Her parents transferred her to the public school system, which did improve her performance. She babysat for neighborhood moms in her spare time. They described her as "marvelous with their children." Then another neighbor living an unconventional life-style turned his attention to Joann. In his forties, Mike lived with his ex-wife, her new husband, and four children—two fathered by each man, respectively.

"Joann spent a lot of time there in her early teen years," the family member said. "The situation there was unsettling. One of the daughters spoke of giving her dad body massages, and Mike told people that he had a crush on little Joann. Things escalated from there. On occasion, Joann came home from there so drunk that she vomited. Mike's disturbing attention to Joann was so blatant that he told her mother that he wanted to take the girl on a trip. The mom brushed off the request. I think that Mike may have been sexually assaulting Joann. There was another incident in which Mike came to her front door drunk, exposed himself, and threatened to hit her with his beer bottle. I often wondered why Joann's mother never called the police or why her father didn't deal severely with the guy."

When Joann was fourteen, she slit her wrists. She survived, but her parents placed her in a residential psychiatric unit for a several months. In the period following her institutionalization, Joann exhibited two different sides to her personality. She could be pleasant and kind. But sometimes, she verbally battered her parents with profanity-laced bitterness and anger over her hospitalization. She told them she no longer wanted to be part of her family and would run away, only to return a day or two later. Such unruliness and disrespect were foreign to her parents, who didn't have the skills to effectively address their daughter's problems. The turmoil took a toll on the family, especially Joann's father, an overweight smoker.

The conflict boiled over one afternoon when Joann telephoned her dad at work. She began swearing at him. Later that day, he suffered a heart attack and died. The family was thrust into financial distress. Joann's mother abandoned the battle to control and guide her daughter.

Following her father's death, Joann was arrested in Milwaukee when she was sixteen. A family member believed fast money had lured her into a situation resulting in a charge of prostitution. But's it's likely that a sinister force plaguing the region factored significantly.

A few months after her arrest, Joann called her mom from the Milwaukee bus terminal. She wanted a ride home. The mother did not drive, so she contacted a cousin, who drove out and found Joann disheveled and dirty. Joann's return home was followed by a visit from two FBI agents. They wanted to question her about being taken across state lines. Joann would not talk, but the agents had their suspicions.

During the 1970s, police morals squad detectives and FBI units were investigating a Kenosha, Wisconsin-based multistate prostitution/human trafficking network that recruited teen girls. One of the regional leaders was Danny Harris, better known as Danilo "Chico" Artez, a thirty-year-old smooth-talking con man. The targets of the network were "dispirited and impressionable" runaway girls from small towns across seven states, from Minnesota and Wisconsin to Arkansas and Pennsylvania. Artez operated out of Kathi's Sauna and Massage Parlor in Monona, Wisconsin, just outside of Madison. There he would meet the girls and speak sweetly and convincingly about making them stars as models or exotic dancers. In reality, he forced them into the sex-for-pay racket. An enforcer, along with trusted prostitutes in their late teens and twenties, recruited and transported the girls and maintained discipline for Artez. He required that the girls cater to him as if he were a king.

"Chico made us light his cigarettes," Vicky Sherman recalled. "Whenever you hear his fingers snap, you better be there with a match. We had to bathe him, dry him off, cut his finger and toenails, and lay out his clothes."

When the emotional manipulation and domination failed and he was denied, Artez would burn the girls with cigarettes or beat them to gain compliance. In 1972, a federal grand jury in Milwaukee indicted him and fifteen ring members. Later that year, two prostitutes who were charged but ready to cooperate with FBI agents, were murdered. Their killers were never brought to justice. By the time the Artez operation was brought down and he was heading to prison, Joann Maniscalco had left home and met Glenn Scott.

* * *

Indeed, Sasha Scott was not the only teen who believed her pimp loved her. And by fall 1975, two years after they met, her estranged husband was chasing her with a gun.

When Richard Henkel heard the gunshot, he backed up his car then raced forward up an incline. When he crested the hill, he saw Sasha on the ground. She had blood on her leg, and Scotty was standing over her, gun in hand. Henkel pulled up and exited his car.

Glenn put the gun back in his waistband and spoke rapidly. He told Sasha that he did not shoot at her but that the gun had a hair-trigger and had gone off accidentally while he was running. He pleaded with her to believe him. When Glenn saw Henkel approaching, he pulled out his gun and ordered him back into his car. Meanwhile, several residents heard the gunshot and commotion and ran out of their homes. Glenn walked back toward his car. Sasha got up and got into Richard's car. He took her back to the apartment as Glenn drove away.

Sasha was crying. She had fallen on the cement and scraped her knees. It was just past two in the morning, and she phoned Suzanne at the Court Lounge. When they hung up, Suzanne told Joey DeMarco and his enforcer, Chuckie Kellington, what happened. The three of them sped out to Chatham Crane. Kellington, who utilized a variety of firearms, was armed with a hunting revolver with a scope. While Suzanne tended to Sasha, the three men circled the apartment complex to ensure Glenn wasn't stalking his wife.

During the next several days, Glenn repeatedly tried to contact Sasha. And she kept avoiding him. He tried calling her at Henkel's apartment, but Suzanne ran interference.

"Scotty would call over to Suzanne's apartment," a friend recalled, "and there was always a reason why he wasn't able to talk to Sasha. Suzanne would say that Sasha was sleeping or she was out to the store, and Scotty just wasn't able to get through."

Glenn asked the friend to intervene and tell Sasha that he only wanted to talk with her. He was worried about her being on drugs all the time. And he wanted to reiterate that he didn't shoot at her, but the gun had a hair-trigger and went off accidentally.

"At first I really didn't like the idea of calling over to Suzanne's," the friend said. "I didn't feel at ease about those people, but Scotty kept asking me. So eventually, I called over there and got the same response that she was sleeping or couldn't get to the phone."

"I don't know what to do," Glenn told the friend. "I want her back, and I love her very much."

Sasha, to be sure, had had enough. She wanted Glenn dead. At the Court Lounge, she informed a friend and Mafia associate of her desire. Later, Sasha informed Richard of her plans. She said Glenn had a life insurance policy, she was the beneficiary, and she planned to use the benefit to pay for his murder. Henkel was intrigued by the scheme, even though Sasha did not know the exact value of her husband's policy.

The next time Glenn called the apartment, Richard spoke to him. He brought up the subject of life insurance and asked

Glenn if he had a policy on himself. Richard sensed Glenn was suspicious, so he said he only asked because he knew Scotty, like him, had a criminal record. Glenn said that his insurance benefit was $18,000. Later he told a friend that he was worried about the inquiry and said he was carrying a gun everywhere.

Another pal of Scotty's knew of Henkel's dangerous reputation. "Dick Henkel was the wrong guy to pull a gun on," he told Scotty.

In September 1975, Sasha Scott and Suzanne Dixon scheduled an appointment at the apartment with an insurance agent. They wanted to buy $100,000 worth of life insurance on Glenn Scott. The agent became suspicious when they asked whether Glenn had to know about the policy. He refused to consider the application.

A week later, a contract killer called the apartment looking for Sasha. Suzanne answered. The hitman, an associate of Richard's, disguised his voice because he had previously spoken to her. This time, he didn't want Suzanne to know it was him. Sasha took the phone call, and they discussed her needs and his services.

Then she went to Richard. "What should I do?"

"That's up to you," Henkel said.

Richard overheard Sasha speaking by phone to the hitman again a few days later. She agreed to his fee of $20,000 and gave him the green light.

One morning, four days before Thanksgiving, a couple in their midtwenties arrived at S&S Stables to ride. Glenn Scott's nineteen-year-old stable hand met them. They heard Scotty's television on in the house but could not locate him. Finally, they entered the barn and the cluttered tack room and office area. There they found Glenn Scott sprawled on the floor and obviously dead. Someone had fired so many small-caliber bullets into his head that even the coroner could not provide an exact count.

CHAPTER 8

The package had traveled two thousand miles into Canada to reach the Vancouver, British Columbia, home of George Chatzispiros, a recently retired restaurateur. The sender, or senders, had wrapped it in brown paper and used a stencil to print the return address—the "Greek Amer Assoc" on Fifth Avenue in Pittsburgh. It was addressed to George's twenty-year-old son, who worked as a security guard and was not home. It was Sunday, and the postal worker knocked on the front door to announce the special delivery.

George came out of the house, followed by his nine-year-old son. The boy was excited and snatched the package from his father. George took it back. The delivery man left, and George brought the parcel inside and into the family den. He unwrapped the outside paper. Inside was a cardboard box sixteen inches long, ten inches wide, and five inches deep. George opened the box as his wife and eager son looked on. Inside was a small attaché case. When George clicked the latch and started to raise the lid, an explosion ripped through the room. The blast mortally wounded George and seriously injured his wife and son.

The investigation into the bombing had barely commenced when George Chatzispiros died in the hospital. His wife's arm was severely damaged. The son lost several fingers.

Vancouver investigators worked with US Postal Service inspectors in Pittsburgh. They tracked the origin of the package bomb to an Oakland neighborhood post office and located the clerk who handled the transaction. She recalled the transaction because the female customer had discussed rates for the international delivery. Using the clerk's description, a police sketch artist drew a likeness of the woman; it was distributed to Pittsburgh newspapers but produced no solid leads.

Vancouver cops could not determine a motive for the Chatzispiros attack. It would be five years before two acts of brutality in two countries emerged as crucial pieces of the same puzzle.

* * *

It was 1976, and Richard Henkel's pals from Philly were on the run. Dogged law enforcement officers finally caught up with Junior Kripplebauer and Bruce Agnew. The burglars were convicted of heists in Texas, and each was sentenced to six years. Both men decided that life on the lam was preferable to incarceration. Prior to reporting to prison, Kripplebauer jumped bail. Agnew followed. And they headed for Pittsburgh. Henkel helped the fugitives get settled in a cabin in Canonsburg, a half-hour drive southwest of the city.

Meanwhile, Henkel was working at Jeff's Bar located on South Main Street in the west end, a half mile from the Ohio River. The joint was run by his friend Mike Mullen, a former Pittsburgh firefighter. Jeff's became a frequent gathering spot for the Henkel/Kripplebauer network. They would meet periodically to discuss potential scores. According to Henkel, Kripplebauer wanted him to participate in the robbery of Lee's Trading Post, a jewelry store located in Pittsburgh's upscale Jewish neighborhood of Squirrel Hill. Since it catered to wealthy clients, they assumed the shop

THERE'S MORE BODIES OUT THERE

would be stocked with high-quality merchandise. Kripplebauer wanted Henkel to kill the jeweler, but he declined the job and instead recommended Allan Frendzel, a weathered-face drifter with roots in Chicago. Henkel introduced Frendzel to Kripplebauer and Agnew, and he agreed to the job. Henkel told Frendzel that he would provide him with a .22 pistol and silencer. Apparently, Frendzel had another agenda.

"Allan was at my apartment when I gave him the gun and silencer," Henkel recalled. "When I took a nap, he stole seven hundred dollars off my dresser. Later I found out he was an FBI informant. Allan pulled out of the score then told the FBI something big was going down in Pittsburgh. But he didn't know where because Junior didn't give him the location of the score yet."

Instead of going in with guns and robbing the jeweler, Kripplebauer decided to burglarize Lee's Trading Post at night. After several weeks of planning and using another Henkel associate—a skilled alarm man from Youngstown, Ohio—Kripplebauer and crew hit Lee's. The high-end jewelry they pulled out eventually netted $600,000 after being sold to a "fence," a middleman for stolen property.

After the Lee's Trading Post score, Kripplebauer left Pittsburgh for Los Angeles. Jack Siggson had relocated to LA in order to escape the heat after fighting a Philadelphia arrest for narcotics trafficking, loansharking, and possession of stolen guns. Bruce Agnew stayed behind and moved in with Henkel at the Chatham Crane Apartments.

Sometime during this period, Richard Henkel read a magazine article about a kidnapping. And he got an idea.

* * *

Persons raking in illegal cash often become targets of tax evasion investigations. In early 1977, the Internal Revenue Service began an investigation into the prostitution and pornography empire of George Lee. It was undoubtedly the subject of conversation when Lee had dinner with Nick Delucia and a female massage parlor employee. Afterward, on that frigid evening, two men ran up and shot George four times when he was walking to his Cadillac. Lee died in the hospital. One rumored motive had him cooperating with the feds. That would have made him a liability for higher-ups in Pittsburgh organized crime. A second theory had the hit on Lee originating within the pornography network in Cleveland.

As the months progressed and detectives made little progress in solving the murder, lines of ownership within George Lee's former sex network got messy. Authorities believed Nick Delucia and Tex Gill were vying for control of the lion's share of the empire. Mel Cummings also wanted a piece. But someone wanted him out of the picture. And he knew. Several months after George was killed, Mel headed home in his jade-green Mark IV. Even if he had had his revolver on him instead of in the trunk, it would not have mattered. He had just turned into the parking lot of his apartment building when a sniper's bullet cracked off and pierced a side window. The assassin was on target. But the steel post of Cummings's headrest mount shattered the slug and spared him a fatal wound.

Anthony "Bobby" Pugh, a manager in the Delucia/Gill network, wasn't so lucky. As the holidays approached, he grew increasingly worried. One day, he told his girlfriend he was afraid for his life. Several weeks later, someone he likely knew emptied a revolver into his head. An incarcerated informant pointed cops toward a thirty-four-year-old Delucia relative. The suspect was arrested. But a few days after bonding out of jail, he died. An autopsy determined the cause to be heart disease. Detectives didn't have to wait long to find the next piece in their emerging massage parlor racket puzzle.

CHAPTER 9

On December 23, 1977, downtown Pittsburgh traffic was heavy as usual on the chilly afternoon. The ground was snowless, but a frosty wind whipped at the faces of pedestrians. The nice and naughty Gemini Spa girls milled around the waiting area. They paused when the door opened and the Yellow Cab driver entered. He was making a delivery. Another gift for Sasha. The other girls walked away. No present could top her upcoming trip. A well-off client was taking her on a two-week post-holiday break to Florida. She and her sponsor were leaving the following day.

Sasha accepted the parcel, and the taxi driver exited. The package was a bit big for a jewelry gift box. It was wrapped in white paper and had an attached card. Sasha opened the envelope.

"It's from Randy," she announced to the girls. They all whooped and chuckled. He was one of Sasha's regulars. One of her kinkier regulars. Freaky Randy. During downtime, the girls often shared stories of their most eccentric clients.

Sasha tore away the paper. It was a jewelry case. The kind with a hinged top that a girl would have on her dresser to hold numerous pieces. It was jewelry, after all. But a whole boxful? Maybe the box itself was the gift. Sasha lifted the lid.

The *BOOM* reverberated throughout the building. The noise and pressure wave jolted occupants. On the street, the intense burst of destructive force overhead stunned pedestrians. The taxi driver / delivery man, returning to his cab, was showered with broken glass. A woman fell to the sidewalk. Then she got to her feet and ran. A blind man clutched a stranger's arm. An off-duty fireman passing by pulled his truck over and got out. People were pointing up. Over the Slack Shop, three windows had been blown out. White curtains billowed in the wind, and someone mentioned a gas explosion. The fireman, followed by two Good Samaritans, ran inside. He directed occupants outside then ran up a stairwell.

On the second floor, smoke and dust filled the air. Three Gemini girls, one with an injury to her eye and one with a leg injury, plus the male receptionist, staggered out of the spa. They approached the elevator. The fireman redirected them to a rear stairwell and asked whether anyone was still in the spa. One of them said there was a girl inside. The fireman ran into the Gemini through the haze. He quickly located the focus of the blast—blown-out windows and a jagged opening in the floor. And near the hole, next to the mangled Christmas tree lying on its side, was a gruesome scene—the broken and blackened body of Joann "Sasha" Maniscalco Scott.

Firefighters, cops, and reporters descended on lower Liberty Avenue. Detectives and bomb squad investigators briefly interviewed the Gemini employees. It was clear that the explosion was caused by a bomb disguised as a Christmas gift. They started examining the scene to rule out a secondary device, search for other victims, and find the source of the blast.

Detectives chatted briefly with police commanders. Sasha Scott's slaying followed those of Bobby Pugh, George Lee, and the attempted rub-out of Mel Cummings. It was becoming apparent that there was a war over control of Pittsburgh's massage parlor sex businesses.

One hour after the Gemini bombing, police were called regarding a suspicious package at the residence of Nick Delucia. Cops rushed to the scene. Someone had placed a parcel outside his front door. It was wrapped as a Christmas gift in pink paper. A bomb squad technician used a rope to slowly pull the package to their reinforced disposal trailer. A wood plank propped against the disposal unit would serve as a ramp to slide the suspected bomb up to the opening. Despite the technician's gingerly efforts, the package dropped to the ground. Police officers, firefighters, and residents, at a distance, were stunned, frozen, and wide-eyed as they anticipated the blast. Seconds ticked by, but there was none. Bomb technicians picked up the package and placed it in the disposal unit. Later, when they opened it, they found a gift of cheese and dried sausages. Reporters sought comment from Nick Delucia. He wasn't talking.

News reports jarred the peace and joy of Christmas Eve and Christmas Day by detailing the shockingly violent death of Sasha Scott. Mayor Richard Caliguiri was determined to do something. The day after Christmas, he obtained a court order for police to close five massage parlors immediately. Attorneys Allen Brunwasser and Paul D. Boas, representing some of the owners, called a foul. They argued denial of due process. A state appeals court judge quickly agreed and reversed the hastily issued order. Despite the setback, Caliguiri promised to keep the heat on.

Meanwhile the Maniscalco family had Sasha's body returned to Wisconsin. The pastor of their parish in Whitefish Bay refused to have her funeral mass there because of her past. Instead, it was held at another Catholic church in Milwaukee.

In Pittsburgh, Suzanne Dixon was deeply disturbed and saddened at the murder of her best friend. She hosted a memorial service and paid for food and refreshments. It was well attended.

As the investigation continued, some law enforcement authorities weren't sold on Sasha's murder being the latest salvo in a war to control the sexed-up rub joints.

"The bombing would have been a stupid move for someone seeking control," said one lawman. "That brutal killing brought down the angry wrath of every politician, judge, church, and police official in the county."

Attorney Boas likewise had doubts. He suggested that someone may have directed the bombing at Sasha Scott for personal reasons.

As detectives continued their investigation, they ruled out Sasha's client Randy as a suspect. However, it was apparent that her killer, or killers, knew her well enough to know that she had a client by that name. Likewise, cops eliminated the cab driver as a culprit. He said he was outside the airport when given the package by a man who appeared to be wearing a disguise, including a fake beard.

* * *

Richard Henkel continued working at Jeff's Bar. When Mike Mullen, the primary owner, had to serve a prison stint for fraud, Henkel bought a 50 percent interest.

"Jeff's had a decent breakfast and a good lunch," Henkel recalled. "Our afternoon business was pretty good, but at night I closed early—at midnight—unless there were still customers. There was usually no business after 10:00 p.m. One night, I let three guys in right before closing because they wanted a six-pack. They asked if they could have a draft beer while I cleaned up. Like a dummy, I said okay. They sat at a table and started drinking while I got ready to close. While I was almost done cleaning up, I overheard one of them say, 'I think he is scared.' I walked behind the counter, and the young guy stood up and said, 'How about another beer?' When I told him no, he said, 'I think I'll help myself.' I reached under the counter and took the gun out. His buddies told him that I had a gun, and the kid sat back down. I told them to leave. And they did. If I had to shoot one, I would have shot all three, for there wasn't going to be a police report, and I wasn't going to jail for shooting one.

"Another night, I was at home when my friend Harry, who I hired as a bartender, did shoot a guy. The bullet went through both his legs. When I got to the bar, I closed up and told Harry to go home. I told two other people to leave and keep their mouths shut. Then I found the bullet. The next day I sent word to the guy that got shot, that if he kept his mouth shut, I would take care of his medical expenses. But that night, his two huge brothers came to the bar. They told me they wanted Harry's address. When I refused to give it, one of them said, 'Bars can catch fire.' I told them both if there's a fire, some people will die. There was no fire, they never found Harry, and the guy that he shot never talked."

When Mike Mullen was released from prison, Henkel returned his 50 percent stake in Jeff's to him. Richard continued working at the bar but concentrated on various money-making interests with his network of badfellas—which, according to a police source, included Edgewood borough cop Gary Small and Henry "Red" Ford, a scrapper with an assault conviction who lived above a bar a few doors down from Jeff's.

"Henry had red hair, but I never called him Red," Henkel said. "We were tight. I saw him almost every day, and we would go out to eat a lot. But I never told him, Mike Mullen, or anyone else that I killed anybody. I never had the urge to brag about work, and I did not share it. I was also that way about banks, etc. Henry is a stand-up guy, and I respect him. He was a tough guy, and during fights, he bit two guys' ears off. But he is a good guy."

According to a police informant, Henkel operated numbers gambling and Barbut games on the South Side. Barbut (also Barboute or Barbooth) originated in the Middle East and was brought to the US with Greek immigrants. Similar to craps, it's a fast-paced dice game involving two players betting against each other and trying to throw winning combinations of numbers.

The numbers racket, or illegal lottery, is a form of gambling involving the random selection of numbers. The player wages a small amount of money for a shot to win a much larger amount. Writers collected nickel and dime bets at any location where somebody in charge agreed to accept bets. It could be a house, barbershop, bar, market, or somewhere populous like the General Motors assembly plant in Lordstown, Ohio. In the 1970s and 1980s, Pittsburgh mobsters held sway over thousands of Lordstown workers infected with the bug to wager fifty cents for a shot to "hit the number" and rake in some cash.

"Gambling is a game for suckers," an old operator said. "But the suckers keep coming . . . You can't stop the gambling spirit."

State governments recognized the tremendous source of revenue from the gambling spirit. Once legislators created lottery commissions, the state-sponsored numbers wagering was here to stay. Smaller illegal operations faced takeover by better established and more powerful networks.

Henkel's crew had their own loan-sharking business. He bankrolled the operation. Clients who failed to meet their obligations were subject to threats and assaults from his crew.

"They had planned to give them a beating if the customer gave them too many excuses," a police source said. "But they didn't want to hospitalize them at that time because they wouldn't get paid. They felt that putting them in the hospital, or worse, could come at a later time if the beating didn't suffice . . . [Sometimes when] I was in the company of Richard Henkel at his home, Gary

Small would come over and give him large amounts of cash. I took this to be collection money."

The mechanics and income from Henkel's loan operation paled in comparison to his next scheme.

CHAPTER 10

In 1977, several months before Sasha Scott's murder, Richard Henkel hired Debbie Gentile to help at Jeff's Bar.

"A guy I knew recommended her," Henkel said. "He told me Debbie was a good cook, so I hired her."

With an additional employee, Richard could devote more time to the legitimate business he had recently started to sell jewelry and gemstones. Jack Siggson had a similar business, and both men bought from some of the same wholesalers.

Debbie Gentile was born Deborah Kelber and lived in Pittsburgh's Lawrenceville neighborhood. When she was in high school, she had a child. She and the father married, then Debbie dropped out of school. Two years later, after her husband joined the Marines, they divorced.

"They just married too young," Debbie's brother said. "There were no hard feelings. They just had different goals."

In recent years, the single mom with reddish-brown hair struggled financially. She bounced around tavern jobs as a bartender or manager. A family member described her as a carefree, well-liked young woman who would do anything for people. And soon, she was working for Dick Henkel.

Around that time, Richard Henkel conceived a bizarre plot. His coconspirators included Jack Siggson, Red Ford, Gary Small, and Roy Travis—the Canadian whom Henkel had met during his prison time for bank robbery. Travis had been paroled shortly after Henkel. The plan was as creative and comprehensive as it was devious. The victim would be a person of prominence and wealth but one who routinely drove alone. Travis, an electronics expert, had engineered a small device to be covertly wired into a car's ignition system. Once the unit was in place, Henkel and his crew, following behind, could transmit a signal to shut down the engine. They would then kidnap their victim and fit him with a bomb set to detonate in several days. The device would be locked on so that one would need very specific technical instructions to remove it safely. Next, the kidnappers would lock the victim in a specially designed van hidden from public view. Finally, when they received the ransom of $5 million in hundred-dollar bills, Henkel would reveal the victim's location and provide instructions to deactivate the bomb.

Sometimes, the conspirators held discussions at Henkel's apartment. Planning continued into 1978 when Suzanne Dixon learned she was pregnant. She was thirty-two years old and had recently been fired by Joe DeMarco. A short time later, building planners razed the Court Lounge as part of Golden Triangle development. Suzanne took a job waitressing at a restaurant in the Mount Washington neighborhood. Meanwhile, whatever weaknesses he exploited, Richard Henkel—the cunning psychology student—somehow wormed his way into Debbie Gentile's life.

* * *

Henkel and Gary Small started working on bomb components for the kidnap plot. According to a police source, Small supplied the explosives. As an officer of the Braddock District Sportsmen's Association, Inc., the cop had access to sixty-one acres of prime hunting property in Westmoreland County. On one occasion, Henkel, Small, and Jack Siggson detonated dynamite and plastic explosives there as a test.

The final phase involved selecting a victim. Henkel's crew decided on Art Rooney, owner of the Pittsburgh Steelers. When Junior Kripplebauer learned of the plot, he wanted in.

"Henkel's intricate extortion plan impressed his co-conspirators," wrote author Allen Hornblum in *Confessions of a Second Story Man*. "According to Junior, Henkel examined every aspect of the undertaking, even going so far as to calculate how much five million in one-hundred-dollar bills would weigh and how many bags would be needed to hold the alluring bundles of cash. Additionally, he had a lead-lined box built into the van to disable any tracking devices the FBI might try to conceal in the money. He even planned to notify the Army Corps of Engineers to be ready for instructions to remove the bomb around Rooney's neck after the exchange took place."

As planning continued, with the addition of Junior Kripplebauer, there was concern about Art Rooney's age. Some in the group felt there was a risk of the seventy-seven-year-old suffering a heart attack during the kidnapping. They needed a younger victim. They considered Rooney's son but ultimately decided on businessman Edward Ryan, owner of the Ryan Homes residential construction empire. But there was a problem. None of them had ever seen a picture of him.

Ryan owned horses that raced at the Meadows Racetrack, a half-hour drive from the city. Jack Siggson and Henry Ford spent several days driving around the area to spot Ryan. On one occasion, Siggson and Gary Small went to Ryan's house in the evening. They hid in the darkness and watched through a window, but there were too many people there and they could not determine which one was Ryan.

Meanwhile, the FBI caught up with Junior Kripplebauer, and they were closing in on Bruce Agnew. The two convicted heist men faced many years behind bars.

* * *

In May 1978, something apparently changed between Richard Henkel and Suzanne Dixon. A police source said there was tension between her and Debbie Gentile. Suzanne needed money and wanted a new place to live, but Henkel would later claim that was false.

"Suzanne and I never split up, and she never even knew Debbie."

Dixon told a friend that she had received several threatening phone calls. A day later, she went missing. Henkel made a missing person report a day after that, then he telephoned Jack Siggson. Richard told him that he had been in San Diego visiting his brother and would see him soon.

On the afternoon of Saturday, May 27, a twelve-year-old boy was riding his bicycle on Fifth Avenue in New Kensington, eighteen miles northeast of Pittsburgh. As he passed an Oldsmobile Cutlass parked near Sixth Street, he flinched at a stench. The boy pedaled home and informed his father, who called the police. New Kensington cops arrived and recognized the god-awful odor. They forced open the trunk. Inside they found the bloodied and decomposing corpse of a thirty-something woman. Detectives located a man's wristwatch in the car.

Meanwhile, in Los Angeles, Siggson had not heard back from Richard, so he called Robert Henkel, who informed him that Richard had been in San Diego but returned to Pittsburgh because something had happened to his girlfriend. The murder was covered on the front pages of the city's newspaper.

The next day, Henkel phoned Siggson and told him Dixon had been murdered and someone had butchered her. Henkel said he suspected it was a message to him.

An autopsy revealed the victim to be Suzanne Dixon. And she was pregnant. Later, after interviewing family members, they determined that her diamond engagement ring was missing from the body.

Her killer or killers had shot her in the head seven times with a small-caliber weapon, stabbed her seventeen times, and slashed her throat. Her body lay undiscovered for six days.

Suzanne had confided in a friend the night before she was last seen alive. "I have life insurance, and Dick Henkel is the beneficiary. I'm worth more dead than alive."

Suzanne had two policies with her parents as beneficiaries. According to Henkel, she changed them and made him the beneficiary "because she loved me."

As Westmoreland County detectives started their investigation, they had Richard Henkel on their short list of suspects. And they were very much aware of Suzanne's connection to Sasha Scott, whose murder by bomb was only five months old.

"Henry Ford was visiting me when a Westmoreland detective and a Pittsburgh detective came to my apartment and wanted some more information about Suzanne and my alibi," Henkel recalled. "I let them in and left the door open. A young boy named Danny lived upstairs and played with my son when he came every other weekend. The mailman left a package below the mail boxes and Danny saw it. He saw the door was open and said, 'Mr. Henkel, the mail man left this package for you.' I told him to put it on the table and thanked him. As I went to the package, the two police officers jumped up and moved away. As soon as I saw the return address, I knew what it was. One of the detectives as asked me if I was expecting a package. I lied and said no. They left without asking anymore questions."

Even Henry Ford was concerned about the parcel's contents. He asked Richard what he was going to do with it.

"I told Henry it was empty beer cans from Arizona that people sent for my son's collection. If I thought it was a bomb, it would of went into the freezer until the battery was drained."

Suzanne Dixon's mother and father buried their daughter then filed an appeal with the insurance company. They argued that they, not Richard Henkel, should receive Suzanne's death benefit.

As the homicide investigation continued, detectives traced the watch found in the car to Henry Ford. When they questioned him, he claimed Suzanne had broken her watch so she borrowed his.

"We never bought that story from day one," said a cop. "Suzanne had working watches in the apartment."

The case remained unsolved. Meanwhile, attorneys for Henkel and for the Dixon's met with insurance company officials. When it was learned that Henkel was not the one who had been paying Suzanne's life insurance premiums, the hearing ended and he was awarded the $123,000 in benefits.

* * *

On an evening in July 1978, Richard was talking with Henry Ford at his apartment. Debbie Gentile had recently moved in with Ford. It was 6:45 p.m., and she was getting ready to start her 7:00 p.m. shift at Jeff's Bar a few doors down the street.

"Henry and I were talking, and Debbie interrupted us," Richard said. "I told her to butt out. She started getting in my face and screaming 'This is Henry's apartment!' Her spittle hit my face and I slapped her. She screamed that she wasn't going into work. I told her, 'You're done.' I had to work the shift. She came into the bar twice that night and said that she was sorry and that she wanted to work. I told her, 'You're fired.'"

An acquaintance once described Debbie as someone you could not convince was in danger. But, a couple months after Suzanne's murder, she was distraught over her relationship with Richard Henkel. Family members pressed her for information because they could tell she was fearful, but she was reluctant to share details. "I'm into something with persons who know a lot of big people," she told her brother.

By August 1978, Debbie was desperate and paralyzed with fear. She sought the services of a psychologist and told him, "I'm afraid I will be murdered because of the things I know about my boss."

CHAPTER 11

In the fall of 1978, Richard Henkel had a serious problem.

"A guy telephoned Jeff's Bar and threatened to kill me," Henkel said. "He gave a goofy nickname to the barmaid. I didn't know anybody by that name, but I called my friend Harry. He told me it was Billy Rethage."

Wilbert "Billy" Rethage was a skinny drug-dealing hoodlum who was a close associate of burglar John "Jackie" Boyd. After Boyd and Rethage robbed a bookmaker of $5,000, Henkel's friend Harry shook them down. He said the bookie was Henkel's friend and they had to pay Harry the money back.

"Billy was mad because he was forced to pay Harry five thousand dollars that they stole from the bookmaker. I didn't even know about it when it happened! Harry was just using my name to shake them down for the five thousand. Billy lived and loafed in Mount Oliver, a small Pittsburgh borough. I shot up there and went in every bar hunting for him and leaving messages with my phone number."

According to Henkel, Jackie Boyd visited Jeff's Bar to intercede for Billy.

"I wasn't there, but he talked to bar owner Mike Mullen and asked for me to give Billy a break. 'It's too late,' Mike told him. 'Dick doesn't take threats lightly.'"

* * *

At the end of 1978, Debbie Gentile relocated to Los Angeles. Despite her fear of Henkel, she still sought his help. He told her that he would have Jack Siggson help her find work and a place to live. Henkel telephoned Siggson and told him Debbie needed help. Siggson and his wife had just bought a new home in Garden Grove, California, in Orange County outside of LA. They had not yet moved in, but the house had an extra room. Henkel telephone Siggson and he agreed to help Debbie.

In early 1979, Richard Henkel left the Chatham Crane Apartments in Banksville, where he had lived with Suzanne Dixon. He rented an apartment in Ross Township adjacent to Pittsburgh's northern border, and used large amounts of cash to buy jewelry. He had recently lost a bid to purchase a diamond for $30,000.

Back in California, Debbie Gentile was staying with a cousin in Whittier, just outside of Los Angeles. As instructed by Henkel, she contacted Jack Siggson. His wife was expecting their child, and he was preoccupied with moving. Additionally, Siggson was financially stretched from defending himself in the Philadelphia drug and weapon case. He continued to sell jewelry, including at the Long Beach Naval Base exchange. Siggson had been in the new house with his wife for only a few days when Debbie called.

"I can't help you in any way right now," Jack told her.

"But Dick said you would help me," she said.

"Try to get a job on your own. If you don't, give me a call in a few weeks. If I'm better organized, then maybe I can help you."

When Debbie called Henkel and told him that Siggson could not help her, Henkel immediately telephoned Siggson. "Jack, isn't there something you can hire Debbie to do? Maybe help you unpack? It's important."

"Well, we do need help around the house. And with the new baby—"

"Good. I'll talk to you more about it next time I'm out there."

Jack called Debbie and told her he had changed his mind. The following day, she arrived at his house, and he put her to work with housekeeping to help his pregnant wife.

Henkel flew out to Los Angeles, met with Debbie, and gave her cash to open a bank account.

"Debbie called me and asked if I would back her to sell gold jewelry at a flea market on weekends," Henkel said. "It was only a couple thousand dollars."

As Richard instructed, Debbie signed blank deposit slips and gave them to Jack Siggson. Two weeks after Richard returned to Pittsburgh, he flew back to Los Angeles. Before disembarking, he grabbed a copy of the in-flight magazine. Richard rented a car, drove to the Captain's Quarters Motel in Anaheim, and got a room. Jack met him there. On the way to pick up Debbie, Richard told Jack about a life insurance policy available from the Airline Passengers Association.

"It's a quick way to pick up a lot of money," he said. "And I'll pay you fifty thousand for your help."

Richard and Jack picked up Debbie at her cousin's house and returned to Henkel's motel room. They sat around talking about Siggson's new house and baby while Henkel flipped through the in-flight magazine.

Debbie told Richard she needed a car. "She asked me to loan her one thousand dollars. I said okay but she would have to sign a loan note."

When Debbie wasn't looking, Richard slipped the life insurance applications between the pages of the magazine. Next, Henkel turned the conversation to the jewelry business, discussing Gentile settling in Los Angeles. Finally, he told Debbie he had good news. In addition to her job selling jewelry, Henkel could hire her as a jewelry courier traveling between Los Angeles and Pittsburgh.

"It's a lot of flying," Henkel said.

He wrote out a promissory note for Debbie to borrow one thousand dollars then pretended to find the life insurance applications inside the magazine.

"You know," he said to Debbie, "we should fill these out for our moms. I'll fill one out, and you fill one out."

Henkel started completing an application, and Gentile followed suit. She asked Henkel for help several times. "I don't know my cousin's address," she said.

"That's okay. Just use Jack's. Jack, give her your address."

Henkel directed Gentile to leave several lines blank including the one marked "Beneficiary." She did not question why. Then he gave her to loan note to sign.

"Debbie never knew what she signed," Henkel would later reveal. "She was tricked."

When they completed the insurance applications, Henkel took them both. Later, he put his mother's name on the beneficiary line for Debbie's application. Then he selected a death benefit amount of $800,000. The Airlines Passenger Association policy would pay if the insured person died in an airplane crash or on airport property.

Before Henkel departed from Los Angeles, he left Debbie's application with Siggson. Then, he ripped up his application and threw it in the trash. Henkel left several thousand dollars in cash with Siggson.

"Give her a thousand for a car," Richard instructed Jack. "And get her started with a small jewelry inventory. And I'll have her write out a check for three hundred forty dollars for the insurance policy."

Back in Pittsburgh, for several weeks, Henkel continued searching for Billy Rethage in response to his threat.

"I didn't know at the time, but Billy had left Pittsburgh and went to live on a farm that his friend Jackie Boyd's father owned in Greene County on the West Virginia border."

In the meantime, in Los Angeles, Debbie Gentile sold jewelry for Jack Siggson and Richard Henkel at swap meets and flea markets. It had been a long time since she felt a sense of happiness and independence. Then she got bad news. Her mother had suffered a debilitating stroke. Debbie wrote to her mom daily about the progress in her new job and the friendly people she was meeting.

* * *

Debbie Gentile was working at Jack Siggson's house when her life insurance policy arrived in the mail. She looked at the paperwork briefly, but when she left, she forgot it. When Siggson came home, he mailed the policy to Henkel, as Richard had instructed him. A few days later, Debbie asked Jack about the policy. He told her he thought it was junk mail and threw it out. Suspicious of Siggson, Debbie phoned Henkel and said Siggson had either hid or done something else with the documents.

Meanwhile, Debbie and her cousin decided they wanted their own jewelry table. Jack fronted them some pieces and gave Debbie two weeks to sell the jewelry. She had some success, then Siggson told her where to buy a tarp-like shelter tent for protection from the sun. He also showed her where and how to purchase wholesale herself.

One of his jewelry wholesalers complained about Gentile's clothing. "She dresses like a prostitute."

In response, Jack suggested to Debbie that she dress more conservatively when working—perhaps in slacks and a blouse.

Once the insurance policy was issued, Siggson realized Henkel was sucking him into a conspiracy. On several occasions, he encouraged Debbie to leave the area. But each time, she would report to Henkel, then, he would call Siggson and accuse him of trying to derail his plans. As the weeks passed, Siggson feared for his own life. He still wanted to distance himself from the situation, so he told Debbie she could no longer work for him. He gave her two weeks to either sell or return the jewelry he consigned to her.

Meanwhile, in Pittsburgh, Henkel had a female associate purchase a round-trip ticket for Debbie to fly from Los Angeles to Pittsburgh on May 17. The reservation would have Gentile returning the following day. He informed Siggson but told him not to tell Debbie until the actual morning of the trip. Henkel said he tried to set up the murder somewhere else but felt Pittsburgh would give him the most control over the situation.

"I think you're foolish for doing this," Siggson told Henkel. "You've been around so many other deaths in Pittsburgh, this might be the straw that breaks the camel's back."

Henkel wasn't fazed. He instructed Jack to accompany Debbie to the airport and let him know if she made any phone calls before boarding the plane.

"I'll be there personally to pick her up," Henkel said. "Or I'll have someone that she knows pick her up."

On the morning of May 17, Jack telephoned Debbie and told her to come to his house immediately. He instructed her to bring her jewelry inventory. When she arrived, he said Richard wanted her to return to Pittsburgh.

Because Jack's car was being repaired, he accompanied Debbie to the airport in her vehicle. As per Henkel's instructions, he stayed with her until she got to the gate for her TWA flight. Siggson sat with her for twenty minutes.

"I know if I go back to Pittsburgh, Dick will kill me," Gentile said.

"Then why are you going?" Siggson asked.

"I have to."

After Debbie boarded the plane, Siggson left the airport. Several hours later, he got a ride to pick up his car.

It was eight thirty at night when Debbie Gentile's plane landed at Pittsburgh International Airport. She was wearing blue capri pants and a short-sleeved terry cloth top. Since she had no luggage, she walked past baggage claim and headed for the terminal. She passed the Alexander Calder mobile floating above, over the giant black and gold compass inlay on the lobby floor, and up the steps to the second level and the adjacent hotel entrance. At the registration desk, the hotel clerk assigned Debbie to room 239. In an adjacent room, several flight attendants were getting settled.

The next day, just after noon, a housekeeper knocked on Debbie Gentile's door.

CHAPTER 12

As a boy, when Robert Payne marveled at his uncle's police car and uniform, a seed was planted. Many years later, after serving as an Air Force military policeman in Vietnam, Payne joined the Allegheny County Police Department. It was a time when the agency was expanding under the leadership of Superintendent Robert Kroner. Payne, a stocky man, served as a patrol officer with various assignments for five years then accepted an invitation to join the homicide division. He was eventually partnered with Detective Mike Lackovic, a curly-haired, six-foot-tall outdoorsman.

Most of the 130 municipalities within Allegheny County had small police agencies with no detective divisions. Instead, they relied on the Allegheny County Police Department to investigate serious crimes. Greater Pittsburgh International Airport, located in Moon Township, ten miles west of downtown, was also under the jurisdiction of the county police.

* * *

When the airport hotel housekeeper received no response to her knocking on the door of room 239, she used her passkey to open the door, announced her presence again, and entered. She stepped into the main section, which featured two double beds. Only one of them had appeared used. As she moved toward it, she noticed a dark stain on the sheets. She stepped further into the room. And then she screamed.

Allegheny County patrol officers arrived quickly. About twenty minutes later, Bob Payne and a team of detectives showed up. Payne and his partner inched their way into the room. Their victim was lying on the floor, faceup, and fully dressed in blood-stained clothing. Her gold necklace and pendant, gold hoop earrings, gold bracelets, and four gold rings were still in place. She suffered dozens of wounds, including a slashed throat.

"It was overkill. That's for damn sure," Payne recalled.

The detectives made a preliminary identification of the body. It was Deborah Gentile, age twenty-seven. They checked for witnesses, but nobody saw anything helpful. Even the flight attendants in the adjacent room heard nothing. The cops processed the room but found nothing, not one fingerprint or any other evidence to connect anyone to the scene other than their victim. After Debbie's body was moved to the coroner's office, Payne and Detective Tom Fitzgerald left the crime scene to meet with her family members, who were eager to tell the cops about the man for whom Debbie worked.

"I think she was more scared of him than liked him," Debbie's brother told officers.

Until then, the detectives had never heard of Richard Edward Henkel. They checked through the FBI's National Crime Information Center and learned he had served time for bank robbery and counterfeiting.

In the days that followed, a pathologist found that Debbie's Gentile's killer shot her in the head three times and stabbed her in the chest, neck, and back over fifty times. Cops and a firearms expert conducted a test in the hotel room. They used 22-caliber blanks and a decibel meter. It confirmed detectives' suspicion: the killer used a gun equipped with a silencer.

Investigators noticed the similarities between the Gentile and Dixon murders. Ballistic testing revealed that the slugs taken from both victims had been fired from the same gun. Since Dixon moved within the rub joint network, police considered that Gentile's murder might have such a connection. But that wasn't the case.

"We have no proof supporting the belief that Debbie Gentile was involved in the massage parlor or prostitution business," said Robert Meinert, homicide inspector for Allegheny County.

Detectives Payne and Fitzgerald decided to visit Richard Henkel. They drove out to Ross Township, a fifteen-minute drive north of downtown. When they knocked on the door of Henkel's apartment, a man who looked to be in his thirties answered. He identified himself as Henkel's nephew and said he expected his uncle home soon. When the detectives asked to use the telephone to call their boss, he let them enter. The nephew sat at the kitchen table while the Payne and Fitzgerald stood and made small talk. Detective Payne noticed a note fastened to the refrigerator.

Call Jack in California.

There was a phone number. Payne jotted it down then used the wall-mounted telephone to call his boss to let him know Henkel was expected home soon. The detectives heard a door open.

Henkel walked into the kitchen.

"A guy was on my phone and another one was standing over my nephew. Since they didn't shoot me or pull guns, I knew they were the police."

Henkel walked over to the phone and pressed the button disconnecting Payne's call. "Who in the hell are you?" Henkel asked.

"We're from Allegheny County Homicide," Fitzgerald said.

The presence of cops in his apartment, two days after Debbie Gentile was found slain, must have rattled Henkel. "Get the fuck out of my house!"

"We just want to ask you some questions," Payne said.

"Put them in writing and send them to my lawyer. Now get out!"

The cops had no choice but to conclude their visit. As they exited the apartment, they heard Henkel lay into his nephew.

"If you ever let someone in the house like that again, I'll break both of your legs!"

Payne and Fitzgerald didn't yet realize it, but they would soon find that Los Angeles held more puzzle pieces than Pittsburgh.

Meanwhile, Allegheny County District Attorney Robert Colville ordered a grand jury probe into organized crime activities, including drugs, prostitution, and murder. Nick Delucia and Joey DeMarco were among those targeted. As a result, Delucia and several associates were indicted for racketeering and income tax evasion. Delucia, referred to by newspaper reporters as the city's "massage parlor king," was eventually convicted and sentenced to five years in prison.

In October 1979, racketeer Joseph DeMarco disappeared. He had recently been released from a prison stint after a conviction for participating in a large gambling operation run by high-level Pittsburgh mobster John Bazzano Jr. On the day DeMarco went missing, he planned to meet with William Herman Johnson, a former bouncer for a Shadyside nightclub called Fantastic Plastic. Johnson was awaiting trial on drug and weapon charges. Cops located DeMarco's vandalized Chevrolet Monte Carlo in a shopping mall parking lot.

A week later, a patrol officer assigned to the airport checked on a suspicious vehicle that had been parked for several days. Because it was backed into a spot against a wall, the license plate was not readily visible. When the officer checked the plate, he learned it was wanted in connection with its missing owner William Johnson. The police opened the trunk, perhaps expecting to find Johnson. And they did find a body. But it was that of Joey DeMarco. Someone had shot him three times. Johnson remained missing. Investigators considered him either a potential suspect in DeMarco's murder or another victim of his killer.

US Attorney Robert Cindrich, a recent appointee of President Jimmy Carter, was riled by the latest murder connected to massage parlor prostitution. "The DeMarco slaying is another example of organized crime flouting the law . . . thumbing their noses at law enforcement. They're not going to continue to perform these murders, victimize these girls, and do it within a stone's throw of the courthouse. I think we've got to prove to them and the public that organized crime is not above the law, and it isn't going to exist without a battle from us."

The DeMarco family had their suspicions about who killed Joey. According to a newspaper report, when Richard Henkel showed up at the wake, family members told him to leave.

* * *

In 1979, thanks to the $123,000 life insurance payout from Suzanne Dixon's murder, Richard Henkel was flush with investment capital. He and his brother Robert bought a townhouse in Hampton Township. Richard paid for most of the house in cash and moved into it later in the year.

According to a *Pittsburgh Press* story by Mary Stolberg, Internal Revenue Service investigators found that in 1979, Henkel bought $48,000 in jewelry, offered $50,000 to buy gold coins, and bid $30,000 to purchase a large diamond. And he paid $14,000 for title to a house in a deal involving a well-known drug dealer. And in an ironic strategy for a convicted bank robber, he maintained multiple bank safe-deposit boxes, ostensibly to protect and hide cash and jewelry.

"I was living good," Henkel recalled. "I went on vacation several times a year to Canada or Mexico. I took my son on vacation. I had a couple of homes that were in my brother Bobby's name. I had good furniture, pretty ladies, and ate at the best restaurants in Pittsburgh and some bad ones."

Late in 1979, Henkel shopped for Golden Triangle office space for his jewelry business. He chose the iconic twenty-three-story Clark Building that was known as "Pittsburgh's Jewelry District" because it was home to dozens of gem dealers and jewelers. The landlord, C. J. Greve, led Richard through a two-room suite of 260 square feet of unfurnished space on the twenty-second floor. Henkel filled out the rental agreement under the name of International Gold Exchange and handed Greve the first month's rent in cash.

"I hope it suits your purposes," Greve said. "It's due to be painted. We can paint it and put your business name on the door."

"No, no," Henkel said. "I don't want anything done. It's perfect."

CHAPTER 13

Detective Bob Payne and his new partner, Mike Lackovic, made slow but consistent progress in the Debbie Gentile homicide. Their first break was the note on Henkel's refrigerator. The phone number led them to Jack Siggson. They checked into his background and learned that the former Philadelphian had served time for shooting and killing a man during a fight years earlier. Next, they interviewed Gentile's cousin in Whittier, California. The deeper they dug, the more the subject of life insurance became a theme. When the detectives learned of the $800,000 life insurance policy on Gentile, Payne contacted the insurance company. They were ready to issue payment, but he convinced them to hold off.

The detectives worked with the insurance company to get copies of paperwork and addresses. They were convinced that Siggson was lying about his contact with Gentile on the day she left Los Angeles for Pittsburgh. District Attorney Robert Colville would use the powers of a grand jury, including secrecy, immunity, and subpoena authority, to investigate the far-reaching case. Siggson's name was one of first to be placed on the witness list.

Meanwhile, in Los Angeles, Siggson needed cash. He appealed to Henkel. After he flew in for a meeting, Richard was ready to lend Jack $4,000. But there was a catch. He wanted him to hand-write a note and sign it. Henkel had the wording preprinted.

Dick – if you do not give me $4000, I will tell the authorities that you were responsible for Debbie Gentile's murder.

"The note is to protect me," Henkel told Siggson, "just in case something was to happen to you and your family makes a stink."

Siggson recognized the attempt at extortion and the implied threat. He refused to write out the note. Later, Henkel reconsidered his strategy. He told Siggson he had some jewelry he could have and would mail it to him. Three days later, Siggson received a package. Fearing it might be a bomb, he brought it to his garage then instructed his wife to take the baby and leave the house for a while. Siggson taped a sharp knife to the end of a long pole. From behind protective cover, he used the makeshift tool to slowly puncture and eventually open the package. It was jewelry. He sold it later for $1,500.

Jack was subpoenaed to testify before an Allegheny County grand jury. On Feb 9, 1980, he left Los Angeles for Pittsburgh. Richard picked him up at the airport. When they went to eat, Richard told him the insurance company had not yet issued payment for the Gentile policy but he promised to pay Jack $50,000 as soon as they did. The conversation turned to the upcoming grand jury appearance. Siggson had already retained a Philadelphia attorney to represent him. Henkel insisted on using his own lawyer, and he would pay for it. He handed Siggson five one-hundred-dollar bills. Henkel explained that the attorney wanted to receive payment directly from Siggson. Then, if the subject ever arose, he could legally state he was representing him.

After they ate, Richard drove Jack to his lawyer's office and left him there. Henkel's attorney discussed Siggson's testimony and told him that Richard's mother, Hannah Henkel, claimed she did not know him. This was not true. He had seen her at least twice and talked to her by phone several times. However, the lawyer told Siggson to testify that he did not know Richard's mother. He asked whether Siggson knew that Henkel had an insurance policy on Suzanne Dixon. Siggson did not. The attorney said it was only for a few thousand dollars, but the police were making it a big issue. Before he and the attorney left for the courthouse, Siggson handed him the five hundred dollars. Siggson knew what Henkel was doing. With his own attorney advising Siggson about his grand jury appearance, he would learn what Siggson was saying. As usual, Richard Henkel was maintaining control.

Siggson testified before the grand jury and was questioned extensively about his time with Debbie Gentile on May 17, the day she left Los Angeles for Pittsburgh. He stated he last saw Debbie Gentile at ten in the morning when she drove him to a service station to pick up his car. He denied knowing anything about her life insurance policy. Siggson was also asked about Suzanne Dixon. He knew only that she had been Richard Henkel's live-in girlfriend. While being questioned, Siggson learned from the grand jury prosecutor that Suzanne had life insurance policies worth over $100,000. After testifying, Siggson left the courthouse with the attorney to return to his office.

Meanwhile, Detectives Payne and Lackovic wasted no time in contacting the service station owner in California. They determined Siggson did not retrieve his car until six o'clock at night. The cops conferred with Assistant DA Pat Thomassey, and the decision was made to arrest Siggson for perjury. If they could catch him.

When Siggson and the attorney arrived at his office, Henkel was waiting there. The three men briefly discussed the insurance policy on Debbie Gentile. Then, as requested by Henkel, Siggson waited outside the office. Henkel closed the door. After a few minutes, Siggson heard the phone ring. A few seconds later, Henkel opened the door quickly. The call that the attorney received was from Thomassey. The assistant district attorney wanted to know whether Siggson was there. The attorney told Thomassey he had already left. After hanging up, he told Henkel to quickly leave with Siggson, who soon returned to Los Angeles.

When Payne and Lackovic could not locate Siggson, a warrant was issued charging him with perjury. And as their investigation progressed, they learned from the Airline Passengers Association that insurance paperwork for Gentile had been mailed to Siggson's house.

* * *

On July 16, 1980, Jack Siggson returned to Pittsburgh to surrender on the perjury warrant. Lying to the grand jury, especially during a murder inquiry, could result in prison time if he was convicted. And the fact that Siggson had a murder rap on his record increased his risk. No doubt, he was carefully considering his options. Before Siggson turned himself in, he responded to a request for a meeting from Henkel. Considering his knowledge of Henkel's brutal world, he must have anticipated potential danger. Richard also told Jack he would take him to collect money owed to him by a mutual associate.

After checking into a hotel, Siggson met Henkel at the home of Mike Mullen, the owner of Jeff's Bar. Henkel had told Siggson that Mullen was willing to put up his house to secure any bond from Siggson's pending arrest. And presumably, the purpose of the meeting was to discuss the perjury case. Henkel had already obtained an attorney to represent Siggson in his new case. Richard was waiting outside when Jack pulled up to Mullen's house, a nice-looking bungalow with a two-car attached garage on a cul-de-sac. Richard looked in the car. If he was surprised or upset, he didn't show it. Siggson had brought along his wife, their six-month-old child, and a male friend.

Mike Mullen was not home, but Richard had a key to get into the house. He and Jack sat in the kitchen and chatted about the perjury case while Siggson's wife and friend entertained the child. Ten minutes had gone by when Siggson looked through the window and saw a car pull into the driveway and park behind his car. It was Mike Mullen. Someone was in the passenger seat. Siggson got a bad feeling. He looked closer. The man climbed out of the car.

It was Gary Small. Mullen walked in, entered the kitchen, opened the door to his basement, and turned on a light. Gary Small blocked the doorway to the living room as if to keep every-one in the kitchen. The casual conversation was slowing.

Siggson caught a glimpse of metal under Small's shirt. It appeared to him that the cop was carrying two pistols—one equipped with a silencer.

PART 3

Lead Characters:

Richard Henkel
Ralph Cappy: Allegheny County criminal court judge
Paul Gettleman: defense attorney
Mike Lackovic: Allegheny County Police homicide detective
Robert Payne: Allegheny County Police homicide detective
Kim Riester: special prosecutor for Allegheny County
Jack Siggson: burglar and associate of Kripplebauer and Henkel
Gary Small: Edgewood Borough police officer and friend of
    Henkel
David Smith: Allegheny County assistant district attorney
Patrick Thomassey: Allegheny County assistant district attorney

CHAPTER 14

Detectives Payne and Lackovic obtained traces of phone calls placed between the home of Debbie Gentile's cousin in Whittier, California, Siggson's place in Orange County, California, and Henkel's house in Pittsburgh. These connections strengthened their evidence that the two suspects were involved in Debbie Gentile's murder. And when they learned that Henkel collected $123,000 in life insurance proceeds from the death of Suzanne Dixon, their case came into focus. A governor's warrant, with a request for a high bond, was obtained and sent to California. Orange County deputies went to Siggson's Garden Grove house but found nobody home.

Payne and Lackovic learned from street sources that Siggson was in Pittsburgh. They assumed he intended to surrender on the perjury warrant and were anxious to speak with him. The cops knew Siggson was a key puzzle piece in the Gentile murder mystery and thus was in danger. They began searching Henkel's known haunts like Jeff's Bar. Three days later, the cops still could not find Jack. Pittsburgh authorities feared the worst.

Days earlier, when Siggson visited Mullen's small house with family and friend in tow, he knew he had made a mistake. He was sitting at the kitchen table when he glimpsed Gary Small's silencer, a six-inch-long pipe-like attachment affixed to the barrel of his gun. Jack got up from the kitchen table and headed through the living room and toward the front door. He noticed Henkel move in that direction. Siggson beat him to the door, picked up his child, and walked outside.

He called to his wife and motioned her close. "Under no circumstances go back in the house," he whispered. "Stay outside with the baby."

Henkel followed the Siggson family outside. Then he urged them to go back inside.

"I want the baby to stay out and play," Jack said. He then called his friend outside to stay with his wife. When he went back inside, there was little conversation between Henkel, Small, and Mullen.

"They lost control of the situation," Siggson would later state. "They didn't know what to say. I believe it was just luck that prevented my wife and myself from being killed."

Siggson, his wife, child, and his friend walked away unharmed from the visit. His perjury warrant would have to wait. He quickly left Pittsburgh and returned to his home in Garden Grove, California. He knew he was a major liability but had outsmarted Henkel. At least for now.

CHAPTER 15

One week after Jack Siggson's self-reported close call at Mike Mullen's house, Henkel telephoned Siggson in California. He told him the insurance company had still not paid the $800,000 on Gentile's life insurance policy, but when they did, Jack would receive $50,000. Henkel ended the call with a not-so-veiled threat. "If they don't pay on this one," Henkel said, "I have a husband and wife in mind."

"I hope it's not me," Siggson said.

While Jack Siggson and Richard Henkel were contemplating their respective next moves, the Youngstown, Ohio, Mahoning Valley underworld was bubbling with tension. The latest conflict resulted from the murder two years earlier of mob associate Danny Greene in Cleveland. Those convicted of the 1977 hit on "the Irishman" included Ronald Carabbia. After Ron went to prison, his brother Charlie inherited oversight of the Cleveland Mafia's interests in Youngstown and Ohio's Mahoning Valley.

When Danny Greene was killed, Cleveland burglar Phil "Superthief" Christopher was in prison. Joe DeRose Jr., an associate of the Carabbia brothers, was in the same facility. The two became friends, and Christopher learned of events that led up to the tension in Youngstown.

"When we were in the joint, Joe DeRose told me that Jackie Tobin and "Peeps" Cononico, two Youngstown racketeers, beat him out of his share from a burglary score," Christopher recalled. "He said when he was released, he was going to get even with them."

DeRose was released in 1978 and became Charlie Carabbia's enforcer. But he also started settling personal scores. Some law enforcement officials suspect Richard Henkel was drawn into the conflict through his friendship with Joe DeRose.

"I was close with Joe," Henkel said. "He was generous, a lot of fun, and was great at one-liners. He could have been a stand-up comic. I never seen him drink hard booze or beer, but Joe enjoyed wine. He stayed sober when he worked."

DeRose was the prime suspect, in 1979, when James "Peeps" Cononico and Jackie Tobin were killed. Other murders quickly followed. As the underworld body count ticked upward, key Mafia associates in Ohio's Mahoning Valley had to choose between Cleveland's crew, headed by Carabbia, and the Pittsburgh faction, led by Jimmy Prato and his protégé, Joey Naples.

Phil Christopher was familiar with the Mahoning Valley underworld and made numerous trips to visit DeRose. On one occasion, Joe brought up the recent murders of Tobin and Cononico.

"I told you I'd get even with them, Phil," Joe said.

During another visit in early 1979, Phil Christopher found DeRose at his Youngstown apartment drinking wine with Richard Henkel at nine in the morning. Phil had met Henkel the previous year during an attempted burglary of a jewelry wholesaler in Beachwood, a suburb of Cleveland.

"Joe started talking about a million dollars' worth of life insurance money that Dick was supposed to get," Christopher recalled. "Dick Henkel gave me bad vibes. He was quiet, and there was just something about him I didn't like."

Joe DeRose spoke of other killings in the Mahoning Valley.

"Joe wasn't admitting to any murders," Phil said. "But he made it very easy to read between the lines. He was popping pills and drinking a lot. He was running wild and obsessed with the idea of taking over Youngstown's vending and gambling rackets."

In May 1980, DeRose and his girlfriend were outside their apartment building when shots rang out. A team of hitmen working for Joey Naples, of the Pittsburgh mob, had fired on the couple from a passing car. DeRose was struck in his arm and neck. His girlfriend was hit in the abdomen. When police arrived, they interrupted DeRose trying to stash a 9mm pistol. Later, the US Bureau of Alcohol, Tobacco, and Firearms traced the gun to Gary Small. DeRose and his girlfriend survived their injuries.

Phil Christopher recalled another visit with DeRose. When he arrived at his apartment, Richard Henkel was there and had brought with him two young prostitutes who were lesbians. "Watch this," Joe said to Phil.

The girls started kissing. Then, they performed various sex acts with each other. DeRose and Henkel were amused. Christopher, not so much.

"I wasn't into watching girls kiss and put on a lesbian sex show," he said. "And I didn't care for this Dick Henkel. I thought he was a little screwy from the things that came out of his mouth like collecting insurance from dead people."

After Richard departed with the girls, Phil spent the night at Joe's apartment. The next day, he accompanied Joe to see his boss, Charlie Carabbia, the Cleveland mob representative, at his bar. While sitting in a booth, DeRose opened his jacket slightly and displayed a pistol with a silencer.

"As soon as Charlie comes over, I'm gonna put a couple in him," Joe said.

"What are you talking about?" Phil said. "Quit fucking around, Joe."

DeRose smiled but was silent. Christopher was incredulous that he would joke like that, especially in Carabbia's bar. Then, a few months later, Charlie Carabbia went missing. Cleveland cops found his Cadillac Eldorado abandoned on the west side. According to mob underboss Angelo Lonardo, Jimmy Prato and Joey Naples had Carabbia murdered after they learned he was targeting them. Meanwhile, Joe DeRose tried to stay ahead of gunmen loyal to the Pittsburgh mob. He occasionally left Youngstown and went to Pittsburgh to hide out at Richard Henkel's house.

CHAPTER 16

While Pittsburgh authorities continued searching for Jack Siggson, Henkel telephoned him again. This time his message was straightforward. "If you're not with me, Jack, I will commit genocide on your whole family."

Siggson hung up and called his attorney. He and his family left their house and moved into a hotel to contemplate his next move.

After weeks of searching for Siggson, Detectives Payne and Lackovic received news from their West Coast counterparts. He was alive and had just surrendered to Orange County authorities back in California.

An extradition hearing for Siggson was scheduled for August 25, 1980. Payne, Lackovic, and Assistant District Attorney Thomassey planned to be there. A few days before their flight, they learned that Siggson had obtained a postponement until October 3. The municipal judge released Siggson on his own recognizance but failed to notify the district attorneys in Orange County, California, or in Allegheny County, Pennsylvania.

"I'm just appalled," Thomassey said. "They have a different outlook on the law out there than we do, evidently."

Once again, Payne and Lackovic would have to track down Jack Siggson before Richard Henkel did.

Finally, in October 1980, Payne, Lackovic, and Assistant District Attorney Pat Thomassey were notified that Siggson was in back custody in Orange County. They flew to California to testify at his extradition hearing and meet with him.

"Siggson was worried about him and his family being killed by Richard Henkel," Detective Payne said. "He knew he was in a pivotal position and that he could very easily be murdered. That, plus us wanting to put him in jail for perjury, is what turned him."

Payne, Lackovic, and Thomassey returned Siggson to Pittsburgh by commercial airliner. And using his knowledge and cooperation, the investigators began lifting a dark veil to expose the brutal world of Richard Henkel.

"When we offered Siggson immunity from prosecution for his testimony," Payne said, "he opened up with everything. And we put him in protective custody."

In additional debriefing by detectives, Siggson said Henkel admitted he was a contract killer. His standard fee was $20,000, and he referred to murder as "permanent work." Siggson said Henkel told him Edgewood cop Gary Small accompanied him whenever he did permanent work. Payne and Siggson spoke of the bomb kidnap extortion plot for the first time, and Jack implicated Small and the other members of Henkel's crew in that scheme. Payne and Lackovic were stunned at the additional allegations, especially after learning a fellow cop was being implicated as a contract killer. It was another facet to investigate.

Under the protection of numerous detectives, Siggson testified to a grand jury about the Gentile case. He detailed how he and Henkel set Debbie up to be murdered. He said Henkel told him she knew incriminating things about him. By killing her, Richard would eliminate any problem he might have in the future and also make some money. Henkel considered arranging for Gentile's murder to occur elsewhere but felt he could have more control over the plot in Pittsburgh. Siggson stated that a day after Gentile was found dead, Henkel admitted he had her killed but had a solid alibi. Based on Siggson's new testimony to a grand jury, investigators obtained an arrest warrant charging Richard Henkel with murder.

Meanwhile, Richard Henkel had been unable to reach Jack Siggson for several weeks. No doubt he assumed he had flipped. By October 1980, Henkel had moved to Hampton Township, which was twenty minutes north of downtown. His side-by-side brick-and-frame two-story duplex on West Hardies Road sloped downward, with the front door at street level and the rear door at basement level. The house sat across from St. Catherine Catholic Church and School.

Inspector Charles Mosser, the short and bespectacled new chief of the Allegheny County Police Department homicide division, was concerned about getting Henkel into custody. Did he have explosive devices? Would he fire on police as they approached? Would he attempt to flee? Would Henkel's associates be at the house? Clearly, it would be a high-risk operation.

Mosser decided to be patient and gather intelligence. He wanted surveillance on Henkel and his house for several nights before executing the arrest warrant. On Monday, October 20, his team quietly positioned an undercover recreational vehicle, manned by two detectives, in the parking lot of St. Catherine's. Tom Fitzgerald and Herb Foote had the first overnight watch.

Henkel spent that evening at Three Rivers Stadium watching the Oakland Raiders defeat the Pittsburgh Steelers. It was approaching midnight when he was about to pull into his driveway. Instead, he noticed the RV and whipped into the school lot. Fitzgerald saw the car coming, and both detectives moved away from the windows. Henkel pulled right up beside the vehicle.

When the detectives realized it was him, they stepped back to conceal themselves. They watched Henkel exit his car. He walked up to the RV and peered into the windows as the cops remained motionless. A few seconds later, Henkel got back into his car and pulled out of the parking lot and into his driveway.

For three days and nights, the police monitored Henkel's residence. They used binoculars to peer into Henkel's window. At times, they caught glimpses of a second male.

On October 23 at 6:45 a.m., Inspector Mosser's team began staging near the school. Support team members included a sniper, a K-9 officer with a dog trained to sniff for explosives, and another K-9 patrol unit in case Henkel tried to flee on foot. In addition, the acting chief of the Hampton Township Police Department and an agent from the US Bureau of Alcohol, Tobacco, and Firearms were present.

The sniper set himself up in a prone firing position on top of a county police Ford Bronco in the school parking lot. He covered the front of Henkel's house as the arrest team moved into position. Fitzgerald, armed with a shotgun, was sent to the rear of the house with a uniformed officer. Bob Payne, also toting a shotgun, joined Mike Lackovic and the ATF agent at the front door.

At 7:15 a.m., Inspector Mosser used a bullhorn to call Henkel outside.

"Richard Henkel. This is the Allegheny County Police. Come out your front door with your hands up!"

There was no immediate response.

"We know you're in there," Mosser shouted.

Still no response.

The inspector called on the radio and instructed the teams to make entry. Fitzgerald and his partner shoved open the back door leading to the basement. As Payne's team kicked in the front door, Fitzgerald climbed the steps to the kitchen where Henkel had positioned an ironing board to block the basement door. He ran from the kitchen, and as he approached the stairwell to the second floor, he was met by the muzzle of Payne's shotgun. The officers ordered him to the ground. Henkel looked back toward the kitchen, but Fitzgerald was there. Sandwiched between two shotguns and otherwise by officers with pistols, Henkel made another attempt to climb the stairwell. Several officers pushed him to the ground, handcuffed him, and searched him. Richard was in distress, and he had a request. The timing and shock of the raid pushed him beyond capacity.

"I need to use the bathroom."

The officers were concerned for their safety. Mosser instructed them to check the rest of the house for other persons. There was nobody.

While passing through Henkel's bedroom, Bob Payne noticed the grip of a pistol sticking out from between the box spring and mattress. It was a 9mm handgun. Henkel, as a convicted felon, was prohibited from possessing a firearm. Payne's observation of the gun in plain view created probable cause for request of a search warrant to look for additional evidence. After letting Henkel use the bathroom and change clothes, several officers hauled him off to Allegheny County Jail while a third officer prepared an affidavit for a search warrant. A few hours later, a judge issued the warrant, which was rushed to Henkel's house, and a team of officers began a regular search.

They located a second weapon—a .25-caliber pistol—under Henkel's bed. In another section of the house, officers confiscated a cassette tape of Henkel's phone conversations with Suzanne Dixon, Debbie Gentile, and Jack Siggson. In addition, they found a telephone interceptor device apparently used to make the recordings and also numerous safe-deposit keys—two with the numbers filed off. They also located the last will and testament of Henkel's mother.

The detectives seized small boxes of electronic components in the garage, apparently sent to Henkel from Roy Travis in Canada. There were wiring diagrams and instructions, cassette tapes, and an antenna with a mount for temporary attachment to the gutter of a vehicle. Investigators believed the components were related to the bomb kidnap plot.

Paul Maryniak was a tenacious *Pittsburgh Press* reporter with well-placed government and street sources.

"It was my habit to be ahead of just about any other reporter in the Allegheny County Courthouse," Maryniak recalled. "Consequently, I received a tip about the arrest and was able to be in Judge Robert Dauer's courtroom when Richie Henkel was hauled in for arraignment. What struck me was how nonchalant he was, like being charged with first-degree murder was no bigger a deal than a traffic ticket."

Maryniak broke the story of Henkel's arrest for Debbie Gentile's murder, and his colleagues scrambled for comments. Officials were delighted. Robert Kroner, the Allegheny County police superintendent, announced that Henkel faced homicide and criminal conspiracy charges. District Attorney Bob Colville revealed that witness Jack Siggson was in protective custody. He praised the work of Detectives Payne and Lackovic, who continued to debrief Siggson.

C. J. Greve, the owner of the Clark Building in which Henkel rented an office, monitored the extensive news coverage. He had already filed for foreclosure since Henkel had not paid his August and September rent payments.

Meanwhile, Henkel's preliminary hearing began. Paul Gettleman, a popular defense attorney who routinely wore a ponytail in court, represented him. Gettleman's wife, Eleanor, was also a lawyer, and they lived on a small farm where they raised cows. Patrick Thomassey, a skilled and passionate DA who was often assigned tough cases, argued for the state in the courtroom of District Justice John L. Musmanno.

A squad of Allegheny County police officers served as a security detail, since it was Jack Siggson's first public appearance. Other cops stood guard near Henkel, still in pretrial custody, wearing blue jeans and a white T-shirt. Courtroom visitors had to pass through a security checkpoint with a metal detector.

Bob Payne was one of the state's first witnesses. The detective testified about the evidence found during the search of Henkel's house, particularly the two handguns. The 9mm pistol, police had learned, was registered to Gary Small. It was the second time police found a firearm registered to the cop and in the possession of a known criminal. Payne spoke of finding Hannah Henkel's will.

"The majority of items [in the will], including $800,000 from Debbie Gentile's insurance policy, were left to Richard," Payne said. He noted that Mrs. Henkel had three living sons and that the will had been dated two days after Debbie Gentile's murder.

Jack Siggson spent a full day testifying in the witness chair. Defense attorney Paul Gettleman repeatedly attacked his credibility, a routine strategy for defense lawyers who faced a soiled prosecution witness. He brought up Siggson's conviction, twelve years earlier, for murder. He got him to admit he served as a drug courier for Henkel and he lied to a grand jury early in the year.

"He is not a witness to be believed," Gettleman said.

"I lied because I was scared," Siggson said. "Knowing Mr. Henkel and his reputation . . . if I did not go ahead and help him out [with setting up Debbie Gentile to be killed], I would be murdered."

While Henkel slouched in his chair, Gettleman addressed Siggson's relationship with the accused killer. "Did you consider Mr. Henkel a good friend of yours?"

"I don't think Mr. Henkel had any friends," Siggson replied. "He once told me, 'I like you as well as anybody, but if someone gave me money to kill you, I would kill you. But I would not hurt you.'"

The testimony struck a nerve. Henkel "leered and laughed," Linda Wilson for the *Post-Gazette* later wrote. "At times he shook his head in apparent disagreement with Siggson's statements. When Siggson testified about the kidnap extortion plot, Paul Gettleman noted the absence of this information in the original grand jury testimony."

Patrick Thomassey countered. "Siggson feared he would also be killed if he told authorities about the extortion plot earlier than last month because four others who knew of it have been brutally and mysteriously killed."

The preliminary hearing took four days—two of which consisted of Siggson's testimony. Judge Musmanno ruled there was sufficient evidence for Richard Henkel to stand trial for the murder of Debbie Gentile. The case was assigned to Judge Ralph J. Cappy. Pat Thomassey announced he would seek the death penalty. Consequently, Henkel was held without bond.

News reports told about the bomb kidnap plot and Siggson's testimony implicating Gary Small.

"We are evaluating possible criminal action against both Mr. Henkel and Mr. Small," said District Attorney Robert Colville. He was not ready to provide details.

Small, a ten-year veteran, was known by many as a good cop. Borough officials and residents referred to him as an "all-American boy" and "a nice guy." A few days after the Edgewood mayor digested the stunning accusations against his patrol officer, he sent him a letter of suspension. Small denied the claims but offered little explanation. The borough council hired Michael J. Reilly, a former district attorney, to coordinate an investigation into the officer's conduct.

Meanwhile, landlord C. J. Greve was increasingly concerned about reports of missing persons connected to Henkel. Accompanied by two sons, he went to inspect his rental unit. They slipped a master key into the knob, but it wouldn't turn. Henkel, in violation of his lease agreement, had changed the lock and failed to notify Greve.

The three men forced their way into the office. They found the two-room suite empty except for a closed duffel bag in a corner. Greve unzipped the bag. The contents dumbfounded them. Wrapped inside newspaper were four new military-style gas masks. The men notified the police, who were unaware Henkel had a rental unit. The presence of the gas masks remained a mystery for decades.

In the meantime, Paul Gettleman challenged the discovery of the 9mm handgun in Henkel's house. He argued that police should not have gone to the second-floor bedroom. Though recent federal case law had created a "protective sweep" exception to the search warrant requirement, Pennsylvania had no such provision. Gettleman reasoned that since the weapon's presence formed the basis for the issuance of the search warrant, the court should exclude all evidence seized from Henkel's house following his arrest. Assistant District Attorney Pat Thomassey said police had the right to perform a sweep of the house because they feared Henkel's violent tendencies.

In a hearing on Gettleman's motion, Inspector Mosser testified he had information from a police informant that Henkel made a threat against the district attorney.

"I'm not going back to prison," Henkel reportedly told the source. "And when the investigation is over, I'll have a package for Mr. Thomassey."

Police and prosecutors knew that "a package" was underworld common speak for a bomb.

In additional testimony, Inspector Mosser spoke about a 1975 police report made by Small's ex-wife during the brief period that Henkel lived with the Smalls. She alleged her "former husband had been involved in drug dealing and told her he had killed someone. She said Small once ordered her to leave the house for a few hours, and when she came back, she found blood in the basement."

According to Bob Payne, Small countered the police report by filing emergency psychiatric papers on his ex-wife alleging that she was a danger to herself or others. It was a nasty ruse. As a law enforcement officer, Small knew how to word such petitions successfully. Any future allegations by his former wife against him would be met by suspicion due to the record.

Meanwhile, a judge ruled police and prosecutors could open three safe-deposit boxes traced to Richard Henkel but only in his chambers. If they were expecting to find stacks of cash, a murder weapon, or Suzanne Dixon's missing ring, they were disappointed. The boxes contained envelopes and a McDonald's restaurant bag—all empty.

* * *

The first half of 1981 saw several significant developments. In January, attorney Michael Reilly completed his work for the Edgewood Borough Council. In a closed session, he presented his findings. The next day, the council passed a resolution accusing Small of "openly and notoriously" associating with Henkel while knowing he was engaged in a variety of crimes and conspiracies. They terminated the suspended cop from his $17,000-per-year position in a unanimous vote.

Meanwhile, an Allegheny County grand jury completed their investigation into the bomb kidnap plot. Jack Siggson was, of course, their key witness. They indicted Small, Henkel, and Henry Ford. Roy Travis was also charged. Detectives notified Royal Canadian Mounted Police investigators and they started surveillance on Travis in anticipation of a federal arrest warrant.

A few weeks later, Small was out on bond when he arrived at court for a hearing. Journalist Paul Maryniak was waiting to cover the proceeding when the recently fired cop spotted him.

"He walked up to me in the corridor and said, 'Are you that guy from the *Press*?' Maryniak recalled. "He just looked at me with these icy-blue eyes that made me wonder if I was looking at a stone-cold killer. This was the only case out of hundreds I covered as a journalist that had me concerned for my safety."

Later that month, Joe DeRose Jr. went missing. Investigators believed Henkel was involved in some of the Youngstown area slayings attributed to DeRose. And some thought Henkel, even sitting in jail, knew about his Ohio pal's disappearance.

In May, Henkel and attorney Gettleman received good news. After a lengthy evidence suppression hearing, Judge Cappy ruled on the gun found under Henkel's bed.

"Knowing full well the officers' genuine and honest concern for their lives," Cappy said, "this court concludes the law in Pennsylvania does not provide a vehicle in circumstances such as these for the police to 'sweep' a residence for their own protection."

The ruling, which Cappy made with "great reluctance and true remorse," excluded the use of the 9mm handgun as the basis for the search warrant. Therefore, none of the evidence seized under the authority of the search warrant was admissible in court. The inability to present as evidence the electronic components from Canada, their instructions for use, the taped phone conversations, and the .25-caliber pistol was a brick wall for the good guys.

Patrick Thomassey appealed the decision, and the case went to the Superior Court of Pennsylvania.

Meanwhile, Henkel waited. And he schemed.

CHAPTER 17

In October 1981, Henkel was assigned to work in the Allegheny County Jail kitchen when he met James "Sonny" Watson, an associate of Chuckie Kellington, the violent gang member and former enforcer for the murdered mob associate Joey DeMarco. Henkel befriended Watson, and not long after, Sonny approached a corrections officer.

"I can improve your financial situation," Watson told him.

Watson asked the guard to make impression of keys to two gates and a door leading to an outside delivery area. The impressions would be used to cut duplicate keys. The guard notified his supervisor, who then called the police.

Meanwhile, during a visit with his brother Robert, Richard provided information for him to pass along to Mike Mullen.

"When Bobby or anyone else came to visit me, they brought paper and a pen," Richard explained. "And I would have my own paper and pen. Me and my visitor were separated by plexiglass, and I didn't trust the intercom phones for anything I would not tell my local FBI. I would write down my message and hold it up to the window. If it needed to be copied, my visitor would use his pen and paper to copy it."

Richard used this system to provide Robert with a note to give to Mike Mullen. The plan was for Mullen to handle payment to the guard and receipt of the key impression. But unknown to Richard Henkel and Sonny Watson, the guard was cooperating with detectives, who convinced him to play along. They provided him with fake key impressions.

In the jail, Sonny Watson directed the guard to visit Mike Mullen at Jeff's Bar. He did. And numerous detectives waited nearby. The guard walked into the bar, met with Mullen, and gave him the fake key impressions. When Mullen handed the guard $200, the police moved in and arrested him. While searching him, they found a note in his pocket.

Dick was in court and couldn't call. Will call Tuesday. Here is $40. I'll bring the rest in Sunday. If that same guy comes back and drops off the package, and only if he drops of the package, give him $200.

The note contained a phone number that was traced to Robert Henkel's wife. Cops believed Richard Henkel and Sonny Watson would use the key to escape jail. As a result, officials moved Richard to Pennsylvania's State Correctional Institution – Pittsburgh. The facility, located on the city's north side along the Ohio River and comprised of century-old stone buildings, held thirteen hundred inmates. It was better known as Western Penitentiary.

Paul Gettleman argued that Henkel's transfer to the big house, with its much stricter security, hampered his ability to visit his client and also prolonged his workday. A judge rejected the argument.

Meanwhile, in Vancouver, British Columbia, Royal Canadian Mounted Police investigators arrested Roy Travis as the alleged electronics expert in Henkel's kidnap plot. In May 1981, Allegheny County District Attorney Pat Thomassey and Detectives Payne and Lackovic flew to Vancouver to attend his initial hearing. They alleged that Travis had mailed Henkel electronic components for the use of remotely shutting down a vehicle and locking a bomb to a person, and also that he had provided instructions for their use. A request to extradite Travis to the US for trial was filed.

Vancouver officials gave their American counterparts access to files on other bombings. While Bob Payne was flipping through the 1975 Chatzispiros case file, he paused at a US Postal Service sketch of the female suspect who had mailed the bomb from Pittsburgh. He had not seen it before.

"That's Suzanne Dixon," he told a Vancouver detective.

As a result, Canadian authorities took a fresh look at the George Chatzispiros case. They learned that four months before the bombing, a Vancouver department store security officer detained Roy Travis for shoplifting audiocassette tapes. Worried his parole might be revoked, Travis tried to escape, but the officer was stronger than he was and held him for police. The security officer, and the person to whom the mail bomb was addressed, was Chatzispiros' twenty-year-old son. Despite the potential motive, there was no evidence to proceed with charges against Travis, and the tragic case remained unsolved. And when extradition paperwork from Allegheny County failed to meet Canada's deadline, Roy Travis was freed.

Back in Pittsburgh, Allegheny County detectives continued their investigation into attempted jailbreak. Based on the note with the phone number of Robert's wife, the cops executed a warrant to search his Youngstown home. There, Detective Mike Lackovic found another slip of paper similar to the one found on Mullen.

Locksmith can get key cut.

The note contained the serial number of a lock that matched one in the county jail. Detectives obtained an order for Robert Henkel to provide them with a sample of his handwriting.

* * *

In January 1982, Judge Cappy surprised prosecutors and detectives when he dismissed the bomb kidnap conspiracy charges against Henkel, Gary Small, and Henry Ford. He ruled that the statute of limitations had expired because the plot dated to 1977. Prosecutors countered that the scheme was ongoing. Richard Henkel had plenty of time to contemplate his options as rulings, dismissals, refilings, and appeals crawled through the justice system.

In a separate ongoing civil case, Lois Windsor had been unable to file a claim for her ex-husband's $50,000 life insurance benefit. The FBI believed Laurence Windsor fled after they identified him as Henkel's partner in a 1969 bank robbery. There was even a belief that he left the US for England, his birthplace. But thirteen years later, he was still missing.

Mrs. Windsor's attorney applied a section of Pennsylvania law rooted in "specific peril."

The fact that an absentee was exposed to a specific peril of death may be sufficient ground for finding that he died less than seven years after he was last heard of.

The provision covered cases of victims lost in natural disasters, such as an earthquakes or storms at sea. Lois Windsor argued that the specific peril with which her ex-husband met was Richard Edward Henkel.

An FBI agent was among those witnesses who testified. He had tried for five years to track down Laurence Windsor. "I don't believe the man's alive," the agent testified.

Detective Bob Payne testified about Jack Siggson's information regarding Henkel's "violent tendencies," and *Pittsburgh Press* reporter Paul Maryniak spoke of his extensive coverage of Henkel since his arrest for Debbie Gentile's murder.

The irony may have amused Henkel. While the widow fought for a legal presumption of death to collect her ex-husband's life insurance, Richard had already collected insurance on his murdered fiancée and sat in jail charged with murder for life insurance in Debbie Gentile's death.

* * *

On November 15, 1982, the good guys received good news. The Superior Court of Pennsylvania decided to uphold the protective sweep of Henkel's home.

Under those circumstances where police executing an arrest reasonably believe there are other persons on premises who might endanger their safety, we agree that Pennsylvania law should permit a cursory sweep in the interest of protecting officers engaged in the hazardous work of law enforcement. On the facts of this case, however, we reject the use of the protective sweep doctrine to justify the search, since there was no reason to believe that there were persons on the second floor of the house. However, since Henkel himself was attempting to reach the second floor, we uphold the sweep on the basis of the "moveable area of control."

Accordingly, we find that the police lawfully and constitutionally retrieved the 9mm weapon that was partially exposed under a second-floor bed, and we reverse the lower court.

Paul Gettleman filed another motion to get Henkel returned to county jail. He argued that his client needed better access to a telephone to prepare for his trial. When the request was denied, Henkel filed a federal lawsuit arguing that his constitutional rights were being violated. For the time being, Richard would remain at Western Penitentiary. He got a job as a clerk in the supply room where packages sent to the prison were received. Meanwhile, he got chummy with fellow inmate Louis Coviello.

* * *

Time was passing Richard Henkel with a vengeance. Nineteen eighty-three had barely greeted him when Robert Colville's office refiled the bomb kidnap conspiracy charges. Henkel was reindicted. And he wasn't happy about it. During the arraignment, the judge repeatedly asked whether he understood the meaning of "conspiracy."

Henkel said, "No."

"How far did you get through school?"

"I dropped out in the ninth grade," Henkel answered.

"Must have been a lousy education."

"It's a lousy society when you have judges like you."

Henkel was held without bond in the Gentile murder, but the judge bumped his kidnap conspiracy bond from $100,000 to $150,000.

A few weeks later, a federal grand jury indicted Henkel for illegal possession of the handguns found at his house. Robert Henkel and Gary Small were charged with unlawfully providing the weapons to Richard. Then, Henkel learned Allan Frendzel, another inmate at Western Penitentiary, was going to testify as to statements he said Henkel made to him about murders he committed.

Henkel would later claim that Frendzel lied. "Allan Frendzel used old newspaper clippings to lie and connect me to unsolved murders."

Meanwhile, in the federal district courtroom of Judge Gerald J. Weber, the trial for Richard Henkel possessing two handguns was underway. Codefendants Robert Henkel and Gary Small were charged with purchasing the guns for him. US Attorney Judith Giltenboth argued that Richard Henkel utilized his brother Robert as a strawman buyer for the Hampton Township house and one of the pistols and used Gary Small to obtain the second gun.

But when Robert Henkel took the stand, he testified that he owned both firearms. He said he bought the second gun from Gary because Small was having financial trouble. "I knew Gary was a proud man and wouldn't take [a handout]," Robert testified. "So I bought the gun."

Defense attorney Paul Boas pointed out that Gary Small had been childhood friends with Robert. When Richard was paroled from his prison sentence for bank robbery, he said Gary gave him temporary housing as an "act of kindness." Robert Henkel asserted that he owned the house and both guns. The prosecutor countered with records and their star witness, Jack Siggson.

Siggson testified that he saw Dick Henkel with handguns on two occasions. He said his former associate told him about an incident in which he was startled by his reflection and responded by sending a small-caliber slug through a mirror. Siggson stated Henkel was always on the lookout for specific pistols and silencers. Most remarkable of Siggson's testimony was that his former associate once bragged about murdering twenty-eight persons.

Bill Petraitis, an agent with the US Bureau of Alcohol, Tobacco, and Firearms, presented evidence that Gary Small bought eight handguns, including the 9mm pistol found during the search. Small made the purchases during the period that Richard was living with him.

Boas attempted to discredit Siggson. "Did you help set someone up to be murdered in the last three or four years?"

"Yes," Siggson replied.

On March 25, 1983, the jurors made their decision.

"We, the jury, find the defendant, Richard E. Henkel...guilty."

Henkel leaped from his chair as US Marshals moved close to restrain him.

Reporter Mary Stolberg wrote, "Henkel began gesticulating wildly and hurled a stream of profanities at Judge Weber."

Weber, a former US Army captain, didn't flinch and didn't wait for the usual presentence report. Instead, he immediately hit Henkel with the maximum prison term of four years and fined him $20,000 for possessing a firearm as a convicted felon. This prompted Henkel to "spew out another invective."

"Take the creature away," Weber ordered.

The walls of justice were closing in on Richard Henkel. But, as always, he had a plan.

* * *

A jury acquitted Gary Small of aiding and abetting Richard Henkel in obtaining the 9mm handgun. Robert Henkel was found guilty of illegally providing one of the guns to his brother. Judge Weber deferred sentencing. But almost immediately, Robert had other problems. When he exited the doors of federal court, county police officers took him into custody. Police Superintendent Bob Kroner explained that he was arrested after his handwriting was connected to notes found at his house and in possession of Mike Mullen. The notes linked Robert to the 1981 plot to help Richard escape from county jail.

Paul Boas argued for dismissal of the charges. "The only thing we know about Robert is that he wrote these two pieces of paper," the lawyer said. "He was never seen by witnesses. His name never came up at the jail. The only evidence the government offers is there was an alleged conspiracy between Mike Mullen and Sonny Watson and that somehow because Robert Henkel wrote these notes, he is part of this conspiracy. I suggest that my client's 'crime' is that his last name is Henkel."

A reporter tried to interview Robert Henkel, who was out of jail on a bond and staying at his mother's house in Youngstown. He had recently been laid off from his job at US Steel.

"You don't understand the anguish my family is going through," he told the reporter. "I'm asking you again, politely but firmly, leave us alone."

Ultimately, the state jury hung on Robert's escape conspiracy charge. He was sentenced to two years on the federal weapons charge.

* * *

By spring of 1983, Mike Lackovic, Bob Payne and their team members had connected most of the dots in a trail of bodies dating to 1969. They believed Richard Henkel and his accomplices were responsible. The cops had accumulated evidence to suggest Henkel was a serial killer with at least three fairly recent victims including Glenn Scott, Sasha Scott, and Suzanne Dixon. However, there was insufficient evidence to indict any of Henkel's associates for homicide.

Meanwhile, Patrick Thomassey moved on with his law career. The Allegheny County assistant prosecutor had worked the Henkel investigation since shortly after Debbie Gentile's body was found in her airport hotel room. To counter the setback in the now infamous case, District Attorney Bob Colville brought back his assistant DA, Kim Riester, who handled complex litigation before moving to private practice. Riester was assigned to the Henkel case as a special prosecutor. He sought to establish a pattern of killings by Henkel—a "common scheme" of multiple murder victims. If the evidence was allowed, it would be a blow to Henkel's defense.

In a pretrial hearing, prosecutor Riester introduced the bombshell testimony from Wilbert "Billy" Rethage, the drug dealer who reportedly threatened to Henkel in 1979.

"Dick was my lover," Rethage stated. "And I sold cocaine and heroin with him."

Rethage was asked why he was cooperating with the police.

"I thought I was dying of cancer. I wanted to make amends with my god."

Rethage reportedly had a history of psychiatric illness and alcohol and drug abuse.

Years later, Henkel would claim Rethage made false statements in order to help his friend, a burglar named Jackie Boyd, who was recently sentenced to fourteen to twenty-eight years in prison for convictions in a spree of thirty-five residential burglaries.

"Jackie was a weightlifter and a junkie, and he and Billy were great friends and did crimes together," Henkel later wrote. "I didn't know either that well, and I was never in a homosexual affair with Billy or anyone else. That was just another part of the conspiracy that Jackie and Billy put together."

Prosecutors also had the statement of Henkel associate Chuckie Kellington, a key member, with William "Eggy" Prosdocimo and Robert "Codfish" Bricker, of a notorious drug and robbery gang. Henkel had predicted correctly that Kellington would turn federal cooperating witness when faced with a potential death penalty case from the murder of a drug dealer in Florida.

"I warned Bricker that Kellington would rat, but he did not believe me," said Henkel.

In Kellington's statements to cops, he quoted Henkel as telling him, "Insurance companies are good ways to make money.

It may take a while for you to get your money, but you get it in the end."

By this time, Henkel was ready for his next move. He informed his attorney that two fellow inmates would confess to killing Sasha Scott and Suzanne Dixon. Louis Coviello, a twenty-five-year-old former high school football star, had recently been sentenced to life in prison for murder. The other inmate, John Dooley, was serving thirty to sixty years for robbery. Henkel's strategy was a reprise of his previous unsuccessful attempt in 1970, when he convinced his jailhouse pal to take responsibility for a bank robbery but was foiled by his inability to pick a bank teller out of a lineup.

"Smarter than the average convict, Henkel seemed to have no trouble getting inmates to do his bidding through a deft combination of threats, promises, and entreaties," wrote author Paul Maryniak.

Judge Cappy scheduled Henkel and Coviello for a courtroom meeting on the morning of Thursday, April 14. He would advise Coviello of his rights then and hear his testimony directly.

* * *

On Wednesday, April 13, 1983, one of Detective Mike Lackovic's informants told him that several Western Pen inmates, including Richard Henkel, had guns and were planning an escape during their transport to Allegheny County Court or perhaps once they arrived at the courthouse. Lackovic passed the information to superiors, and it went to the district attorney's office and to Eugene Coon, the county sheriff. From there, it was given to the warden of the county jail, who in turn notified a Western Pen supervisor. The warden, George Petsock, was on vacation in Florida, and several top administrators were attending a training seminar north of the city. Instead of conducting a thorough search of Henkel's living quarters, the Western Pen supervisor ordered increased visual inspections from outside the cell. The enhanced observations produced no evidence to indicate a pending escape.

CHAPTER 18

Daniel Kohut, a thirty-nine-year-old divorced father of a three-year-old daughter, was a corrections officer with sixteen years of experience as one of Western Pen's regular unarmed guards. Other than a small folding knife on his duty belt, he had no weapon. Firearms were carried only by a small division of tactical response guards. On Thursday, April 14, 1983, he had just started his workday. Kohut's post for the day was in a small office of the inmate identification section located in the damp basement of the prison's administration building, and adjacent to a storage room. He worked from a desk positioned next to a table. His assignment was to search and prepare inmates for temporary transfer to the custody of other agencies.

Richard Henkel and Louis Coviello were scheduled for the same pretrial hearing. They had passes allowing them to walk unescorted to the administration building. When they arrived at Kohut's workspace, Henkel entered first. He stood next to the table and disrobed as Kohut went through his prison jumpsuit, personal clothing, and personal effects, including legal paperwork. As instructed, Henkel placed his black shoes on the table. Kohut immediately noticed that the insole on one of the shoes seemed built up. He pulled at it, but it was well-glued. He used the tip of his pen to lift the edge, and with his thumb and index finger, he pulled it again. This time the corner of the insole came loose revealing the white grip of a tiny revolver. Henkel snatched at the shoe. For a few seconds, he and Kohut fought desperately to control the weapon.

"Louis!" Henkel shouted. "Help me."

Coviello, a burly weightlifter, moved in. He slugged Kohut in the face and the guard lost his grip on the gun and fell to the floor.

Henkel trained the weapon on him. "Don't try anything, or I'll shoot you in the head."

Henkel handed the gun to Coviello and grabbed his other shoe. He pulled up the insole and retrieved a second identical revolver. Just then civilian prison employee Kostas "Gus" Mastros, a fifty-one-year-old data processing supervisor, walked by. Gus had worked at Western Pen for thirty years and was well-liked by inmates. He peered into the room and saw that Henkel and Coviello were armed with guns.

"Mr. Mastros, please move over to the left and close the door," Henkel said politely.

"Take it easy," Mastros said. "Stay calm."

"I'm sorry this had to happen to you, Mr. Mastros, but that is the way it came down," Henkel said. "You're going to have to stay here."

Henkel grabbed his clothing and shoes, and he and Coviello hustled their captives further back to the storage room off the small office and closed the door, which contained a one-inch diameter peephole but no viewer. The two prison employees were now the prisoners, held by their captors inside the windowless and cluttered room. Eight feet by twelve feet, the storage room was primarily used to temporarily hold the property of inmates. The room held two showers flanking a toilet, a sink, two desks, several wooden chairs, and a table. There was a blue metal shelving unit with shoes, toilet paper rolls, and masking tape. Empty boxes and buckets were scattered about. A wall-mounted phone extension hung near the door.

Henkel pushed one of the desks against the door as a barricade to anyone trying to forcibly enter from the office. He dressed quickly. Henkel eyed a large cage-type clothing locker in which a supply of extra inmate jumpsuits hung. He grabbed the knife from Kohut's belt.

Two guards banged on the door. "What's going in there?" Mastros and Kohut shouted," Stop! They have guns."

The guards retreated, and all went quiet. After half a minute, an emergency alarm blared like a train whistle. Henkel pulled a yellow inmate uniform off the rack. Using Kohut's knife, he and Coviello cut strips of cloth from the uniforms. They used them to bind their prisoners' hands.

The alarm continued shrieking throughout the prison campus. Inmates who had been eating or exercising were interrupted by guards who hustled them back to their cells. A crisis negotiation team was paged. Off-duty prison guards were called in. Local, county, and state law enforcement officers poured into the area. After ten minutes, all of Western Pen's inmates were locked down. The alarm whistle stopped blaring, and it was again quiet.

Henkel's Thursday morning plans had gone awry. The tip called into Detective Lackovic had been accurate after all. Henkel had recently finalized a bold plot to escape. Danny Kohut ruined the plan by finding the hidden gun. And Richard Henkel would not forget it.

"Jesus Christ," Coviello said. "What have we got ourselves into?"

While Louis was wondering aloud at the sudden turn of events, a specially trained team of corrections officers, carrying firearms and wearing flak vests, gathered in the prison basement. A state SWAT team soon joined them. They gathered information on the captors and discussed options, including a forced entry assault through the door or opening a locked trap in an adjacent plumbing room. Outside, a contingent of guards secured the perimeter of the main prison building. And on standby—three ambulances.

* * *

United States Marshals worried that Henkel's move might be part of a broader plan involving retaliation against federal authorities. His inner circle of loyalists on the streets, believed to be as dangerous as he was, might act at his beckoning or perhaps independently. The marshals moved quickly to protect Judge Gerald Weber and prosecutor Judith Giltenboth.

Back at the prison storage room, Henkel and Coviello eyed Kohut and Mastros as they pondered their next move. Without warning, the room went dark. The captors and their hostages dove to the floor.

Henkel, with a pistol in one hand, fumbled in the dark. He felt someone's head. "Is that you, Mr. Kohut?"

"Yes, it's me," the guard answered.

Henkel pressed the muzzle of the gun to his head. "Somebody better get these fucking lights back on before I blow Kohut's head off!"

There was no immediate response. Thirty seconds later, the lights went on. The prison's crisis intervention team—two dozen members—assembled nearby. An administrator reached Warden George Petsock in Florida, and he started making arrangements for return to Pittsburgh. The crisis team went to work discussing the incident. The main negotiator was a psychologist. Other team members included a counselor, a priest, and Deputy Warden Lawrence Weyandt. One of their first objectives was to establish communication with Henkel and Coviello. The dialed the phone in the storage room. Henkel answered. The team explained who they were and provided a telephone extension number. The negotiators asked what the inmates wanted. Henkel hung up the phone.

"I could not think that far ahead," he wrote on a piece of paper to document his thoughts. "I thought they were going to charge in on us and the blood would flow. The POWs would have died and certainly us along with one or two of them."

As the first day progressed, Henkel telephoned the negotiators and said he wanted food sent in. They said they would consider the request but were in no hurry to provide concessions without something in return.

A few hours into the ordeal, Henkel and Coviello realized that prison officials turned off the cold water to the room. They would have shut down the hot water, but there was no local valve. Henkel untied Kohut and Mastros and made them fill several buckets with scalding water from the shower. When it cooled, they could drink it and use it for washing or for flushing the toilets.

Outside, Pennsylvania Department of Corrections spokesman Ken Robinson met with a handful of reporters. "We're constantly trying to keep the communications going," he said. "It's just a matter of trying to take the situation as it goes. They are obviously tired and hungry. We are hopeful for a quick resolution."

The negotiators made sure the hostage-takers knew the obvious. There was nowhere for them to go. Henkel was agitated at the situation. He offered no demands to the negotiators. Meanwhile, SWAT team members in an adjacent room found they could hear faint conversations by listening through a floor-level vent.

They took turns lying in puddles of water until they installed a listening device with recording capabilities.

At night, Henkel ordered Mastros and Kohut to take turns sleeping on the cramped bottom of the clothing cage with the door closed and locked. They had to pull their legs up to their chests to fit.

* * *

By day two, reporters in dozens of vehicles were camped outside Western Penitentiary. Live, top-of-the-hour television news reports, and front-page news stories, covered every angle of the crisis—including Henkel's lengthy history of crime.

"Richard Henkel has fascinated investigators with his apparent ability to manipulate people in a variety of ways," wrote Paul Maryniak.

Said one person familiar with Henkel, "If what they say about him is true, he's the greatest Dr. Jekyll and Mr. Hyde I've ever met."

Louis Coviello's father and sister arrived and hoped to speak with Louis.

"I want my son to come out," Joseph Coviello told a Pittsburgh Action 4 News reporter. "I don't want him to get hurt, and I don't want him to hurt nobody either."

Prison officials would not allow Joseph or his daughter to speak with Louis. Inside the prison, Henkel was tired and hungry, but he did allow a request by Mastros and Kohut for cigarettes. He and Coviello were nonsmokers. Negotiators allowed tactical officers to pass four cigarettes through a peephole. Henkel had Coviello untied both men so they could smoke. After Kohut finished a cigarette, he noticed a paperback book lying on a corner shelf. It was Peter Benchley's just-released novel, *Jaws*, about a killer shark. Kohut lay down in the cage and began reading to pass the time.

Meanwhile, Henkel decided to wash up. He gave his gun to Coviello and stood in front of the sink. "Mr. Kohut, you're not going to try anything while I'm washing, are you?"

"Whatya think I'm crazy or something?" Kohut replied. "You have that big ape over there holding the Roscoes."

After drying off, Henkel made additional written notes. He and Coviello agreed that the informal journal was a good idea to record events in case they were both killed in a raid.

We don't know what to do except afraid to surrender as we feel it means certain death.

* * *

On day three, negotiators finally sent in food—four sandwiches and sodas. After eating, the captors and captives engaged in casual conversation. Kohut spoke of his daughter, who was three years old. Food, which negotiators were slow to provide, became a favored subject. Mastros spoke of the menu at a north side sandwich point he operated with a nephew.

"It's called Ye Allegheny Sandwich Shoppe," Gus said. "We have capicola and pastrami, but our specialty is the Dagwood." He explained that the sandwich, named after the main character in a fifty-year-old comic strip called *Blondie*, was loaded with meats and cheeses in multiple layers.

When things got tense, Kohut tried to defuse the situation with humor. For example, he joked about considering a new line of work. "Rich, if I ever get out of this alive, I'm going to become a volunteer fireman."

A few hours later, Henkel's mood darkened. He grabbed a pen and laid blame on Western Pen officials.

It's almost like they want us to kill us or force us to kill the POW. God, what a waste.

Henkel picked up Kohut's knife. He furiously cut more strips of cloth from the extra uniforms. Coviello joined him, and they tied the pieces together into a makeshift length of rope. They grabbed Kohut and fashioned a noose around his neck. Henkel ordered the guard to climb onto the table against the door and kneel down. Henkel stretched the loose end of the rope and tied it to an overhead pipe. He put his pistol to Kohut's head and instructed him to call out for food to be sent in and for someone to look through the peephole.

Henkel screamed, "I'm not Pavlov's dog!" You can't [ring] a bell and make me eat."

As the crisis team tried to calm Henkel, he threatened to hang Kohut. A Catholic, Kohut quietly prayed the Hail Mary and Act of Contrition. He begged Henkel to point the gun away from his head. He then asked for a priest.

Negotiators said they would consider food. In exchange, they wanted a list of demands. Henkel released Kohut, who, assisted by Mastros, staggered into the clothing cage to lie down. A few hours later, negotiators sent in ham and cheese sandwiches and cake. Mastros knew Coviello liked to eat, so he gave him his slice of cake. An hour later, the mood lightened, and some humor returned. Henkel impersonated a Jewish immigrant trying to sell someone a suit. Later, when he again expressed anger with the negotiators, Kohut suggested he be patient.

"Dick, you just have to hang in there."

* * *

On day four, Henkel and Coviello composed a letter of their demands. They occasionally asked Kohut, a freelance amateur writer, how to spell a word. Coviello wanted a reduced sentence. Both wanted amnesty for taking hostages. When they finished writing, Henkel went to the door. He folded the letter and slipped it underneath to a SWAT team member.

By day five, the situation deteriorated. Coviello and Henkel were no doubt unruffled by the crisis team's failure to take the demands seriously. Henkel brooded about potentially receiving the death penalty in the Gentile case. Coviello lamented his life sentence but still hoped he could someday be released on parole. Both men wondered how much more time they would receive for possessing guns and taking hostages—or whether they'd be sentenced to solitary confinement.

"I don't want any more time tacked on," Coviello said.

Both men grumbled about their situations. They pondered a murder-suicide pact.

"If we kill ourselves, it will be quick and we'll beat the system," Henkel said.

Gus Mastros encouraged communication.

"I tried to engage Richard and Louis in dialogue," he said. "One of their main points was they didn't like the way people talked to them. And they appreciated me always talking nice to them."

Henkel ruminated about his failed escape plans.

"In addition to pistols on me and three handcuff keys that I had hidden in a hollowed-out bar soap," he explained. "And I had someone in a car a few blocks from Western Pen on the way to Allegheny County Jail."

Detective Lackovic's information suggested that in order to escape, Henkel would have had to kill the transporting deputies. An outside accomplice, the brother of one of Henkel's former girlfriends, following behind on a motorcycle, would release him from the sheriff's transport van and race him to a safehouse.

Henkel's account of the plan differed.

"After quietly removing my handcuffs, I would have used the pistols to force them to stop near my friend. I would have destroyed their radios, and me and my friend would have took their guns then locked the guards in the back of the police car."

Regardless of how the escape would have played out, Danny Kohut ruined the plan by finding the hidden gun. And Richard Henkel could not let that go. He decided he would shoot and kill Kohut, and Coviello would kill Mastros, then they would take their own lives. He made another journal entry.

If one must hang, let it be Mr. Kohut. He always treated me like a dog . . . I can kill Kohut with no remorse because he's the one who kept me from my freedom.

Coviello was not comfortable with the plan. When Henkel dozed off, he moved close to Gus. "I could never kill you, Mr. Mastros."

At ten thirty in the morning on the fifth day of the siege, Henkel decided to release Gus Mastros. First, he used strips of cloth to fashion a leash and a collar around Mastros' neck. If the SWAT team rushed in, Henkel would yank Gus back and use him as a shield.

Henkel held on to the leash and allowed Mastros to open the door. The release went without incident, and Mastros walked out into the unusual sight of a heavily armed assault team.

Gus recognized one of the officers. "Give me a cigarette," he said.

Officers provided him with two packs, and he thanked them as they whisked him out of the basement.

"I'm going to church Sunday and light a candle," he said.

* * *

On day six, Richard Henkel was growing desperate. He was raged about things like facing the death penalty or life in prison. He spoke bitterly of the New Kensington mob having moved in on his Barbut dice gambling operation. And despite assurances by negotiators, Henkel remained unconvinced about his safety should he surrender.

I personally am willing to die before I surrender without a settlement that guarantees us that we will not be subjected to daily beatings and spending ten years in the hole.

Henkel and Coviello were keenly aware that their fellow inmates would not look kindly on being confined to their cells for six straight days. Henkel was adamant about the two of them being moved to another facility. Finally, administrators relented. At least, that's what Henkel thought.

Louis picked up the telephone, dialed the negotiators' extension, and spoke briefly with the deputy warden, Lawrence Weyandt.

"We're thinking about coming out," Coviello told him.

CHAPTER 19

Richard Henkel was still worried. When he opened the door, would he be rushed? Would he be beaten or shot? He phoned the deputy warden back. They discussed the procedure for surrendering to the custody of the prison SWAT officers.

Around three in the afternoon, Coviello made up his mind. With revolver in hand, he moved to the door. He bent down, placed the weapon on the floor, opened the door, and slid it out to the SWAT team officers whose weapons were pointing at him. He carefully followed their instructions by placing his hands on his head and slowly walking into their custody. Officers carefully searched Coviello and briefly questioned him. He said Henkel was concerned about being beaten if he surrendered. The negotiators allowed him to use the phone. He told Henkel he was treated fairly when he surrendered.

Henkel still expected the assault team to storm the room. He vacillated between surrender and murder-suicide. Kohut quietly prayed, not knowing whether his captor would suddenly put the gun to his head and pull the trigger. Negotiators tried to keep a dialogue going with Henkel, but he was silent. Instead, he wrote more notes in the journal.

I abhor violence, but one must be what his karma tells him. . . . Plus the fact that I may receive a death sentence or a life sentence from my murder trial, I really don't have anything to live for, so I may take this fucker out before they drop me.

Henkel put his pen down. "I'm going to kill you, then kill myself," he said to Kohut while clenching the revolver.

"Why waste your life?" Kohut said. "It's not worth giving your life. Why kill yourself? Things might be different for you in five years."

From outside the room, assault team members heard a *POP!* They quickly stacked up to make entry.

Kohut shouted, "I'm okay! I'm okay!"

Henkel had accidentally discharged his pistol. The bullet hit a wall.

Kohut was rattled. "I want to see my daughter again, Dick," he pleaded. "I want to see her again, take her to a park, take her to Sea World."

"Don't worry, Dan, you'll see here again."

Weyandt called through the door, "Are you ready to come out?"

Henkel didn't answer.

Weyandt repeated his question.

"Yes," Henkel answered.

Henkel opened the door tentatively and slid the gun on the floor and out to the tactical officer who had him at gunpoint. As instructed, Henkel put his hands on his head, faced away from the officers, and walked backward slowly through the doorway.

Later, Henkel and Coviello were granted transfer to a different institution. But it wasn't a result of their demand. It was institutional policy to move any inmate involved in such a major incident.

"If you are the cause of thirteen hundred inmates being locked up and hostages abused, you should go elsewhere," said Warden Petsock.

State officials working through the governor's office made arrangements for Henkel and Coviello to be transferred to a federal institution within the commonwealth. An hour after Henkel's surrender, a team of troopers walked him and Coviello—handcuffed, in leg irons, and wearing yellow prison jumpsuits—to a convoy of state cruisers. Henkel hid his face as he was buckled in for the three-hour trip east to the federal prison at Lewisburg, Pennsylvania. The facility was selected for its high level of security. Not long after, Henkel was transferred to the Marion federal penitentiary in Illinois.

At Western Pen in Pittsburgh, Warden Petsock announced Henkel and Coviello would be charged with kidnapping. "We gave up nothing. There will be no amnesty."

For the thirteen hundred Western Pen prisoners, the incident wasn't over. Petsock ordered a shakedown—a complete search of each prisoner and cell. The inmates would remain confined to for a seventh day while corrections officers looked for weapons, drugs, and other contraband.

Kohut was interviewed and downplayed his role in encouraging Henkel to surrender. He stressed that his own life was at stake. "A lot of people in Pittsburgh want Henkel dead. I don't want to be known as the guy who talked him out of suicide."

The Pennsylvania State Police and Western Pen officials began an investigation into the response of prison officials to the information about a possible escape and how Henkel acquired two firearms. His assignment as a clerk in the supply room came into question. An outspoken guard suggested the lack of a robust response to the weapon and escape tip had to do with money. "The warden was not present and . . . nobody below him had the guts to call a general shakedown because of the cost," he said. "A lot of people work overtime when you have a general shakedown, and it costs a lot of money."

Tom Seiverling, administrative assistant to the warden, said, "Our information was that the escape attempt would happen on the way to the court hearing . . . We decided to leave it up to the deputies."

Later, Warden Petsock suspended a deputy superintendent for failing to disseminate the tip to subordinates.

During the firearms investigation, Henkel alleged that Dan Kohut supplied him with the handguns.

"I would never do anything like that," Kohut countered. "I would never do anything to endanger the people I work with."

Some courageous Western Pen prisoners refused to accept Richard Henkel's outrageous claim idly. Instead, they implicated Roy Layne, a recently terminated guard. Two inmates testified that they saw Layne pass two packages to Henkel, one of them measuring three inches by five inches. A third said he saw Henkel unwrap a silver gun. Layne had lost his job for selling marijuana cigarettes to inmates. Layne was arrested on numerous charges involving the firearms used in the botched escape.

His sister, speaking to a reporter, defended him. "It's nothing but a frame-up. He didn't smuggle no guns into no penitentiary . . . It's a lot of bullshit. He wasn't even there. He's a good man and a helluva a good provider."

Prison spokesman Ken Robinson said Layne's arrest resulted from an extensive investigation by the state police and officials from Western Penitentiary.

Henkel might have realized his ability to manipulate and subvert the justice system was ending. He and Coviello were charged with attempted escape, kidnapping, assault, and gun violations.

Henkel announced he would act as his own lawyer. Paul Gettleman, his defense attorney in the Gentile homicide, would serve as an adviser. Since acquittal was unlikely, their strategy would rely in part on the defense of "diminished capacity." They would argue that Henkel's ability to reason, when he took hostages at Western Pen, resulted from his stress over confinement and facing the death penalty in the Gentile case. If the defense was successful, it could establish a lesser degree of intent. That could lead to convictions on reduced charges in the prison siege indictments charging Henkel with a firearms violation, kidnapping, making a terroristic threat, and attempted escape.

Meanwhile, Henkel's trial for the murder of Debbie Gentile approached. Due to intense media coverage, Judge Cappy ordered the jury to be selected in Philadelphia. Under heavy security, Henkel was transferred to the Pennsylvania correctional institution at Graterford, a forty-five-minute drive north of Philly. He was placed in solitary confinement.

One of Henkel's first moves was to request that Judge Loran L. Lewis admit him to a state psychiatric hospital for thirty days of observation. The judge denied the motion but did permit a psychiatrist to evaluate Henkel at Graterford. After an initial evaluation, the doctor said Henkel was suspicious of her credentials and he became tearful and agitated. She and a partnering psychologist conducted an in-depth assessment. They testified that Henkel was hearing voices, believed his food was poisoned, and "fell apart" during a three-hour assessment. Neither of the mental health professionals thought Henkel was feigning psychiatric illness. From a legal standpoint, Judge Lewis had little choice. He ruled Henkel incompetent to stand trial and sent him to Farview State Hospital for sixty days of evaluation and treatment.

Assistant District Attorney Christopher Conrad was skeptical. "I think Richard Henkel is the most manipulative person in the courthouse."

Conrad's skepticism was on point. It took Farview mental health experts only eight days to determine that the accused killer was psychologically fit to stand trial. After that, he was returned to Graterford. While Henkel awaited his murder trial, the warden ordered special precautions. He segregated his notorious guest from other inmates and posted a guard outside his cell for most of the day. To occupy his time, he was given a small television in his cell. Two guards had to be with Henkel when he showered. His mail was monitored, and his visitor privileges were restricted. Henkel responded with a federal lawsuit charging invasion of privacy and violation of his constitutional rights. But he still had hopes of escaping. On Monday, January 9, 1984, authorities received an anonymous tip that Henkel had contraband in his cell. Guards searched and found a handcuff key that he had hidden in a hollowed-out bar of soap, and a piece of wire. The guards suggested the wire could be used as a garrote, but Henkel said he was simply using it to get better reception on his television.

* * *

On January 10, 1984, Henkel was brought to a holding cell outside a Philadelphia courtroom for the start of jury selection. Judge Cappy came in from Pittsburgh, as did Kim Riester and David Smith from Allegheny County District Attorney Bob Colville's office. Henkel was now fully represented by Paul Gettleman. Gettleman's wife was assisting since it was a complicated capital case. Henkel asked to use the telephone. He called his brother Robert, and they spoke at length. Then, Richard talked to Paul Gettleman. Afterward, Gettleman asked Kim Riester and David Smith to join him and his wife in a conference room. Henkel was considering pleading guilty to arranging Debbie Gentile's murder.

As always, Richard Henkel had a plan. The attorneys opened the negotiation with basics. The Gettlemans wanted the death penalty taken off the table. Riester and Smith, in consultation with District Attorney Colville in Pittsburgh, agreed to a sentence of life in prison without the possibility of parole; however, Henkel had to admit to involvement in several other murders for which he was suspected. According to a *Pittsburgh Press* story by Paul Maryniak, Kim Riester had the statement of an unidentified person willing to testify that Henkel told him he killed a fellow bank robber. Laurence Windsor's daughter, twenty-one-year-old Heidi Robin Carter, was desperate for information about her father. She had been at the courthouse trying to get information from investigators.

As the plea deal was being finalized, Henkel had several stipulations. His concern, as it was his whole life, was for himself and his family, no matter how warped his methods. He would admit to arranging Gentile's murder, and his involvement in four others, and also help police find the bodies of two of his victims. However, he wanted prosecutors to drop the pending state case charging Robert Henkel with conspiring to help him escape from county jail. And Richard wanted his brother's federal prison sentence of two years for providing him with guns reduced to probation.

"I could not let Robert go to jail," Richard explained years later. "He was taking care of my mother, and he did not do anything wrong except commit perjury for me."

Robert's sentence was out of Judge Cappy's jurisdiction, but he agreed to speak with Federal District Judge Gerald Weber.

Back in Pittsburgh, news of a potential plea deal spread while Riester and Smith sparred with the Gettlemans over details. The lawyers sent draft provisions to Judge Cappy for his acceptance or rejection. The day ended without a final agreement.

Cappy was hopeful that a decision would eliminate the time and cost of a trial. "Everyone worked hard all day," he told a reporter. "The negotiations were very fruitful and involved other collateral matters. I don't want to say what may happen in the morning because it could change between now and then, so keep your fingers crossed."

The following day, the attorneys finalized the plea agreement. Henkel would avoid death row by pleading guilty to his involvement in the murder of Debbie Gentile. The deal required him to admit his participation in Debbie Gentile's murder and four additional slayings—those of Andy Russman, Bruce Agnew, Glenn Scott, and Sasha Scott. The prosecutors had information connecting Henkel with the murder of Laurence Windsor, but he refused to admit any involvement. Laurence's daughter tried in vain to get an interview with her father's suspected killer.

Meanwhile, the state prosecutors dropped the attempted escape charge against Robert Henkel. Judge Weber withdrew the two-year sentence for the federal firearms violation and instead ordered five years of probation with a stipulation that Robert remain gainfully employed.

Richard Henkel claims he offered to provide information about even more unsolved murders and lead police to additional bodies.

"I wanted full immunity" he said. "They refused, and I ended negotiations."

Richard agreed to lead police officers to the burial locations of two bodies. He would not be eligible for the electric chair because those slayings occurred before the Commonwealth's 1976 death penalty reinstatement.

No doubt Riester and Smith were intrigued, but they wanted the names of Hankel's accomplices. Richard was not about to give them up. He would kill an associate. But he wouldn't rat him out. His decision may have had little to do with loyalty. Henkel simply lacked any leverage to bargain for much more than helping his brother and avoiding Pennsylvania's electric chair.

Reporters scrambled for comments. Assistant District Attorney David Smith said negotiations had become "ghoulish" at one point. "We kept throwing out names of people with some connection to Henkel who had been murdered. It is conceivable that the markers and landmarks that Henkel remembered may not be there anymore. As long as he makes a good faith effort, the plea agreement will go through, even if the bodies don't show up."

"The mitigating circumstances supporting the death penalty were loosely tied together," said Allegheny County DA Bob Colville. "I'm not sure we would win even if we went for the death penalty. We might wind up getting only a life sentence anyway."

Judge Cappy was pleased with the deal and set a time to formally accept Henkel's plea in court. "We are saving time and money by not having this trial, and Mr. Henkel can still face prosecution on the other killings."

Defense attorney Paul Boas said Robert Henkel had mixed feelings about his brother's plea. "He told me that he is happy for his wife and children but feels bad because Richard won't get out of prison except in a box."

Bob Payne said Henkel was a "hired killer who turned to killing for personal gain in insurance schemes." "He profited by more than two hundred thousand dollars. The Gentile case was the cause of his downfall, and he was afraid of getting sentenced to Pennsylvania's electric chair."

Post-Gazette reporter Carole Patton was able to get a comment from Henkel.

"What's the difference?" he said. "You're in jail for life or you die. I'm only concerned that my family is healing now. I don't want any disruption in their lives anymore."

In response to the plea deal, reporter Paul Maryniak wrote, "Henkel may be demonstrating the cunning that has made him one of Western Pennsylvania's most feared criminals."

PART 4

Lead Characters:

Richard Henkel
Bruce Agnew: former associate of Richard Henkel
Ralph J. Cappy: Allegheny County criminal court judge
Robert Cindrich: US District Court judge
Paul Gettleman: defense attorney
Floyd Nevling: new head of Allegheny County Police homicide
    division
Robert Payne: Allegheny County Police homicide detective
Andrew Russman: former associate of Richard Henkel
Gary Small: former associate of Richard Henkel

CHAPTER 20

It had been three years since a team led by Allegheny County PD burst through Richard Henkel's doors and arrested him for the murder of Debbie Gentile. Now, on Wednesday, January 11, 1984, the forty-five-year-old stood in a Philadelphia courtroom facing a judge. He had lost weight, and his pale blue leisure suit draped loosely over his body as he clutched his legal paperwork.

"Why are you pleading guilty?" asked Judge Cappy.

"Because I am guilty of conspiracy and murder," Henkel said.

"You have indicated you are guilty of killing Debbie Gentile?"

"That is correct."

"And are you making this plea voluntarily and with the understanding that you have a right to a trial?"

"Yes."

Judge Cappy sentenced Henkel to spend the "rest of his natural life" in prison.

Patrick Thomassey believed Henkel's deal was part of a plan. "He's going to escape. There's no doubt in my mind that's what this plea is all about," the district attorney said.

An anonymous *Pittsburgh Press* source suggested the deal was another example of Henkel's manipulative nature. "For a guy who controlled people to the point that he did, what better way can Henkel continue to command their loyalty than by always holding over them the threat that he will turn them in?"

Robert Burge, brother to Debbie Gentile, was disappointed with the deal. "Debbie was my baby sister, and I loved her very much," he told a reporter. "I wanted to be at Henkel's execution."

Burge pored over his sister's personal effects and letters. He searched in vain for a reason why she got on a plane to Pittsburgh, knowing she was on a rendezvous with death.

"I've lost a lot of sleep over that question," he said.

* * *

Henkel's trial for the prison siege was heard in February 1984 in Pittsburgh, using jurors bused in from Philadelphia. Richard's makeshift journal, in which he made notes during the incident, was introduced as evidence. The jury convicted Henkel.

A few weeks later, Paul Gettleman informed Judge Cappy about specific information that should not have gone to the jury. It came from the makeshift journal that Henkel kept during the prison siege.

Plus the fact that I may receive the death sentence . . . I really don't have anything to live for . . .

Because jurors could infer that Henkel was also facing a capital crime, they could have been prejudiced in their decisions. As a result, Gettleman and prosecutors held discussions to avoid a mistrial in the weeks to come.

In April, seventy-nine-year-old Hannah Henkel died. Richard, now being housed at the federal penitentiary at Marion, Illinois, requested permission to attend his mother's funeral.

"I requested to go to the funeral," Henkel said. "My brother even delayed the service. The feds were willing, but Pennsylvania refused because the funeral was in Ohio. I was angry and hurt that I could not go to see mom."

In July, Henkel was brought from the federal prison at Marion, Illinois, to Allegheny County Jail. He sat with detectives and sketched a rough map indicating the burial locations of Bruce Agnew and Andrew Russman, Henkel's former associates who had been missing for years.

Numerous officers drove Henkel to the general area of Westmoreland County that he had described. They toured the area, but Henkel said he could not get his bearings.

"I was just enjoying driving around," Henkel later admitted. "So, I didn't tell the detectives when I recognized the location. They started getting upset, so when we passed it again, I had an 'aha moment.'"

Inspector Floyd Nevling was in charge of the search. He had recently replaced Charles Mosser as commander of the county homicide division. Nevling and a crew of police officers from Allegheny and Westmoreland Counties, including two K-9 cadaver dog teams, headed out to the target area. It was a swath of rolling hills off State Route 66, south of Route 380, in Washington Township. And it contained the sixty-one-acre property of the former Braddock Sportsman's Association that Gary Small once headed and the sale of which he had been unsuccessful in halting to housing developers. The cops used Henkel's map to try locating Bruce Agnew's grave. But seven years of nature's growth had passed. In other areas, developers started clearing land and, in some cases, had begun construction. The day ended unsuccessfully. Inspector Nevling's team called in an associate professor of anthropology from the University of Pittsburgh to assist.

On the morning of the second day, Dr. Jeffrey Schwartz and Dennis Dirkmaat, one of his top graduate students with a background in archaeology, met the investigators at the police station.

They were briefed, given Henkel's description of the burial site location, then rode to the property with detectives. Dirkmaat was surprised to see that the area was near his childhood home. The search resources included police and fire volunteers, a mobile forensic unit, a bulldozer, and Allegheny County PD's mobile command post.

Shortly after the search began, Inspector Nevling halted the action. He announced the receipt of a new tip. It had nothing to do with the location of a body but instead seemed aimed at discouraging the continuation of a search.

"The information was that one of the bodies had a booby trap placed on it," said Nevling. Maybe a World War II–type mine."

The property owners knew hunters had frequented the area for many years. They doubted the presence or danger of unexploded ordnance. But as a precaution, Nevling ordered the use of an explosive-sniffing K-9 unit and a metal detector. Searchers were undeterred by the alarming information and resumed their duties.

Professor Schwartz and his student put their skills and experience to work by methodically looking for anomalies in the landscape. They carried only trowels, which they kept in their back pockets. Their methods contrasted sharply with the dozen officers wielding shovels and pickaxes in the wake of a bulldozer operator plowing away small trees.

Schwartz offered his advice to Inspector Nevling. "I tried to explain that you don't have to dig a wide or deep hole to find if someone had dug there earlier. This is because the substance, compactness, and texture of the material thrown back into a hole always will be different from that of the area surrounding the hole."

Nevling permitted the bulldozer and pickax crew to continue their assault. Schwartz and his student moved to an adjacent acre.

It was a sloping and slightly more open area with some pine trees and low-lying plants. They crisscrossed the acreage, paused to examine suspicious depressions, and sometimes used their trowels to scrape and poke gently. As a bright sun rose over western Pennsylvania, the doctor-student team stopped for a break and walked back to the parking area. A cop offered access to snacks and a cooler of sodas inside the command post.

Professor Schwartz and his student resumed walking and examining the landscape and vegetation. It was two in the afternoon when Schwartz noticed something unusual.

"I was scanning the ground for what seemed like the hundredth time," he recalled. "I looked up and noticed what, in the shifting light of the early afternoon, was clearly a long depression. It ran parallel to a deer trail in which three saplings, not of pine, were growing side by side. My student saw the same thing from where he was standing, made a beeline for it, and started clearing away the layer of pine needles. We both felt the soil. It was soft. One more scrape, and the edge of the shovel exposed the top of a massive, human, left femur."

Professor Schwartz announced his discovery as previously instructed. Two homicide detectives rushed over. A K-9 team did too—the handler wanting to encourage his partner who had spent hours sniffing the acreage. With its tail wagging proudly, the dog stood over the leg bone. The procedure called for notification of the evidence team. They responded quickly. Some officers talked of digging the area with shovels and then sifting the dirt using a mesh sieve. Dr. Schwartz discouraged them. He explained the benefits of proceeding slowly and letting him handle the retrieval as if it was an archeological dig. Inspector Nevling and the evidence team agreed.

The burial site was suspected to be that of Bruce Agnew. While the professor and student went to work, the search team used it as a reference point to follow Henkel's directions to the grave of Andrew Russman.

Schwartz methodically dug and scooped out loose dirt, exposing more bone. While working, he educated curious cops about the find.

"As the body decomposed, the fill sank," he explained. "Three saplings took root along the length of the grave, taking sustenance from the unusual source of nutrients."

Patience and the assistance of an expert paid off. An entire grave—five feet by three feet and eighteen inches deep, and its contents—a complete skeleton face down, just as the body had been buried—gradually surfaced. Almost no clothing remained. A metal zipper lay near the pelvis. Above that were a half dozen buttons in a surprisingly neat row. Two plastic collar-stays flanked the neck vertebrae, and a gold necklace lay close. And near them, the bullet that caused the hole in the back of the skull.

Inspector Nevling liked to educate newer officers when opportunities arose at crime scenes. So, he summoned them to view the burial site. Officer Burt Cifrulak recalled being surprised by the reddish-brown color of the bones and the relatively good condition of the necklace.

Schwartz measured the skeleton to calculate its height. He made notes of his other observations, such as dental work. Finally, the remains were placed into a body bag and transported to the offices of the Westmoreland County coroner.

Meanwhile, the search for Andy Russman's body continued in vain. No doubt, Inspector Nevling wanted to avoid the security challenges of bringing Henkel out. For the escape-inclined killer, it might have been an opportunity. But as dusk approached, Nevling called off the search for the day, and Russman's grave remained undiscovered.

The following morning at five, two dozen county police and state troopers assembled at the Allegheny County Police headquarters. Several were armed with shotguns and rifles. Outside, one dozen police vehicles were parked in a line and ready for departure. An hour later, during a six o'clock media briefing, Inspector Nevling explained the level of security.

"We have intelligence that Mr. Henkel has associates who might try to kill him using high-powered weapons or explosives or use the same weapons to secure his release," the homicide inspector said. "Henkel himself is a little nervous of explosives. He doesn't want to ride in the first car."

It was a legitimate concern. Henkel had his share of enemies. One well-placed high-powered slug would forever eliminate the threat of the killer incriminating a cohort in murder. Or a victim's family member or friend might be inclined to vigilante action.

Inspector Nevling anticipated difficulty in locating Andy Russman's grave.

"Henkel hasn't been to the area in seven years, and the landmarks he remembered may no longer be there . . . His description of the location was pretty vague. We'll just give it a try. I don't know how far we'll take it."

It was six thirty when the security detail arrived at the county jail to pick up Henkel, who, according to Inspector Nevling, was surprised at their arrival. Wearing a pair of trousers and an olive-green short-sleeve button-down shirt and sneakers, Henkel was thoroughly searched. An officer handcuffed him, and another secured a thick leather restraint around his waist. The belt's integrated front steel ring, through which the handcuffs would be centered, limited the movement of his manacled hands to just a few inches from his belly. The officers placed leg irons on Henkel and then escorted him to a police car for the ride to Washington Township. Three detectives and attorney Paul Gettleman rode with him amidst a caravan of heavily armed police, a command post trailer, a mobile crime scene unit, and a police helicopter overhead. Twenty minutes later, the convoy reached their destination. They pulled up a dirt road into a parking area and formed a base camp. Because Henkel would have to walk a long distance, an officer removed his leg irons.

The arrival of so many cops, especially the presence of a police helicopter flying low, brought alarm to the quiet area.

"You better lock the door," a resident told his wife. "I think there's an escaped convict out there."

Another resident told a reporter, "You see it on the news, but you don't expect to see it in your neighborhood."

When Professor Schwartz exited his vehicle, a detective introduced him to Henkel. Then, accompanied by Detectives Bob Payne and Tom Fitzgerald, several uniformed officers, and attorney Gettleman, the two walked up an uneven dirt drive toward the target land. The group moved slowly and stepped around or over puddles. They were met by the two property owners who were well into completing a twenty-parcel housing development. They helped orient Henkel to changes in the landscape.

Amidst the occasional choppy staccato of the helicopter swooping by and the frequent chatter of police radios, Henkel and Schwartz conversed casually. The doctor found the serial killer to be intelligent and articulate.

At one point, Henkel mentioned he had covered a victim's body with lime. "Is that the best way to speed up decomposition?" he asked Schwartz.

Bob Payne interrupted. "Why, Richard? Are you planning another murder?"

Cops and the killer chuckled. The professor did not.

The officers led Henkel to the location of the first body recovery. From there he identified two old structures left over from the

150

Braddock District Sportsman's Association—a building used as a shooting range and a shed that served as a snack shack. Using the three reference points, Henkel motioned toward the tract of land where he helped bury Andrew Russman. Cops took him back toward the parking area, and Dr. Schwartz and his graduate student went to work. They walked back and forth, looking for anomalies in the ground. Finally, after two hours, they took a break.

Schwartz walked to the parking area and entered the command post to grab a couple sodas from the cooler. Henkel was inside. He was still handcuffed and sitting down across from the cooler. Two officers, also sitting, flanked him. Schwartz turned and bent over toward the cooler. When he reached for two sodas, he felt a tug at his back pocket. The professor turned quickly. One of the guards had pulled out his trowel. The officer casually tapped the point of the edged tool against his palm several times and side glanced toward Henkel. Schwartz understood. He took the drinks and trowel and hastily exited the trailer to rejoin his student.

The search continued as a squad of cops escorted Henkel across the acreage. He frequently paused to get his bearings. But too much time had passed, so he could not locate where he helped bury Andrew Russman after an associate executed him. Inspector Nevling decided that three days, including one with Henkel, was enough. He called off the search and everyone started back toward the base camp.

Henkel turned to Detective Payne to get his attention. Then he looked out over the vast acreage. "There's more bodies out there."

"What bodies, Richard? Who are they?"

Henkel paused. "I won't answer that."

* * *

A few weeks after Bruce Agnew's suspected remains were unearthed, Dr. Cyril Wecht, the renowned Allegheny County coroner, completed his postmortem examination. Then, Coroner Leo Bacha of Westmoreland County confirmed it was Agnew.

Meanwhile, prosecutors wanted to avoid a retrial in the hostage siege, so they offered Henkel fifteen to thirty years in exchange for guilty pleas. The time would be consecutive to his life sentence. (Louis Coviello had since been convicted in the hostage case and sentenced to ten to twenty years.)

Judge Cappy told a reporter, "We're hoping he'll cooperate and save us the trouble of going through another trial."

Henkel had nothing to lose and turned down the plea offer. Consequently, Cappy had to declare a mistrial due to the improper material that went to the jury. A few months later, another jury convicted Henkel again. Judge Cappy sentenced him to twenty-eight to fifty-seven years.

* * *

During Roy Layne's trial, several inmates testified against the former guard. One said he had witnessed an exchange of property between Layne and Henkel.

Later, Henkel approached the man's cellmate. "If he says anything about this transaction, you better get yourself a fireproof suit."

A friend of Richard Henkel's, serving time for murder, also threatened the witness and his cellmate.

"Henkel thinks you seen the transaction," he said. "If any word gets out on them pieces, [your cellmate] is a dead man, and if you're in that cell, you're a dead man with him."

Ultimately, Roy Layne was convicted of several counts in connection with the smuggled handguns. He would serve nine years in prison. Decades later, Henkel would provide a shocking revelation concerning Layne and the smuggled guns.

CHAPTER 21

On Tuesday, January 17, 1984, Richard Henkel was interviewed by numerous cops and attorneys, including his
lawyers, Paul and Eleanor Gettleman. The western Pennsylvania
detectives included Bob Payne and Herb Foote, who the confessed
killer knew from his 1980 conviction for the slaying of Debbie
Gentile. Henkel didn't use their titles but instead referred to the
officers as Mr. Payne and Mr. Foote. A court reporter recorded
the lengthy session in which Henkel provided details about his
involvement in five murders as agreed in his plea bargain.

Bruce Agnew

Not long after the Lee's Trading Post heist, Junior Kripplebauer
left Pittsburgh for Los Angeles, where Jack Siggson had moved.
Then he received disturbing news from back east. Bruce Agnew
"had gone bad" and was cutting a deal. Junior notified friends who
were likewise at risk from Agnew's rumored about-face. One of
them was Henkel. And Richard decided to solve the problem. He
picked up Agnew downtown. They headed out to the gun club
property in Westmoreland County, apparently on the pretense
of digging up cash that Henkel had buried. Richard worked the
shovel first. After a while, he said to Bruce, "It's your turn to dig."

Agnew took the shovel and dug. Five minutes later, Henkel pulled out a .38 revolver and shot him from behind. Then there was a distant *CRACK*. Concerned that someone hunting nearby might wander close and see him, Henkel hastily maneuvered the body into the hole, covered it with dirt, and made his escape.

Later, Kripplebauer and Henkel spoke by phone. "Don't worry about the problem," Dick said. "It's been taken care of."

At the time of his murder, Agnew was reportedly in possession of a large amount of cash, and two 4-carat diamonds.

"I believe Dick killed [Bruce Agnew] thinking he was doing the people he was associated with a favor," said Jack Siggson. "But it probably had more to do with the money and diamonds [Bruce] was carrying. Dick's first objective is money."

Henkel blamed Kripplebauer for Siggson's knowledge of the Agnew murder.

"Kripplebauer told Siggson about me killing Bruce Agnew for him, and he also told his girlfriend, who testified in the bomb kidnap conspiracy."

Before the law finally caught up with fugitive Kripplebauer, Henkel considered killing him.

"Dick said he thought it was the best solution," Siggson said. "He said he would get a thorn out of both our sides, that Junior was only a taker, and that he used people."

When Kripplebauer was ready to move on from Pittsburgh, Siggson gave him five hundred dollars.

"Dick called me on the phone," Siggson said. "He was angry because I sent Junior the money. I believe he wished to keep him in the Pittsburgh area until he disposed of him. When Junior left California and was arrested in New Jersey, it was probably the best thing to happen to him."

Andrew Russman

"I knew Andy since 1960, I guess," Henkel told detectives. "He was going south on somebody—pulling out money that was supposed to be paid to other people. It was money that he was beating people out of, continually coming up short. And the people found out."

Henkel would not go into more detail over concern of implicating others. But detectives learned that Russman was involved in trafficking heroin. His associates reportedly accused him of diluting the drug to increase his profits.

"I called Andy and asked him to meet me," Henkel said. "I picked him up by myself in my Plymouth Valiant near his house on the South Side. It was very close to South Side Hospital."

Henkel said he drove Russman to meet with a third individual. He would not reveal his name to police, but detectives believed they knew his identity. Henkel said there wasn't much talking when they reached the destination. And he did not describe the type of location.

"We come in and I was behind [my accomplice]," Henkel told the police. "Andy was in front of him. [My accomplice] pulled out the gun and shot him. Three times, I think."

Henkel and his never-identified associate wrapped Agnew's body in a large cardboard box, carried it to a vehicle, drove to the sportsman's club property in Washington Township, and buried it.

Glenn Scott and Joann "Sasha" Scott

When Glenn Scott called Richard Henkel after pulling a gun on him, it was too late.

"Scotty wanted me to know about the stolen weapons," Henkel told detectives. "He was, like, trying to be friends with me again, and he had a bunch of stolen rifles and pistols. He asked if I was interested in them, and I told him yes. I says we will come out and get them a couple nights later . . . I figured if he pulled a gun on me and got away with it, next time he might actually shoot. He shot at Sasha, even though he says the gun went off accidentally."

Later, Henkel told a reporter, "Once he pulled the gun on me, that was it for him. I didn't look at it moralistically. I just felt that he threatened to kill me, and I'd kill him before he did. The insurance was just, like, a bonus on the guy."

Henkel explained to investigators that the plan to murder Glenn Scott was a "screwy coincidence." He went to meet with the other hitman.

"I'm going to do it anyhow," Henkel told him. "To be a race on, we might get in each other's way."

The contract killers came to an agreement and formulated a plan. They would visit Glenn Scott on the pretense of purchasing the stolen guns then take care of him permanently.

"We went out to S&S Stables. We go into the house first," Henkel said. "Scotty says the guns are in the barn. We follow him into this office or hard tack room with bridles and saddles. I had my gun in my waistband. A .22 revolver. An 8-shot. Scotty turned his back to me. I just started shooting him in the head. I reloaded and shot him some more because I was angry."

As part of their plan to confuse investigators, Henkel and his unnamed conspirator loaded most of the rifles into their car. Then, they stopped on the West End Bridge and dumped them into the Ohio River. They knew the police would learn that the weapons left at Scotty's barn were stolen.

"The police would go in circles," Henkel hoped of the red herring tactic. "Whoever was connected to the theft of the weapons would be connected to the killing."

Two days after the murder, Henkel accompanied Sasha to S&S Stables to retrieve saddles, sports equipment, and Scotty's Manpower records.

"We had them for a while," Henkel said of the records. "Sasha thought they was going to be part of the estate because there was a lot of money involved. Scotty had two sets of books—what he was billing and what the county was billing. So, after I saw what was going on, I destroyed them."

A few weeks after Glenn Scott's murder, Sasha received his life insurance benefit. Richard was there with Suzanne Dixon when the hitman called to instruct her how to deliver his payment.

"The person called Sasha on the phone," Henkel said. "Suzanne and me were there. He directed Sasha to put the money in a bag, take Suzanne's car, and go down to the Banksville Shopping Center. She was to put the twenty thousand dollars underneath the driver's side of the seat. He wanted Sasha to go into the Kroger's or Stephen Richard's store and be gone for a half an hour.

"Sasha couldn't drive, so I took her down there. She put the money under the seat. We got out, went in the store, and waited. When we came back, the money was gone."

According to Henkel, Sasha was never aware that it was him, accompanied by the hitman she retained, who killed her husband. Henkel's associate cut him in for $5,000 for pulling the trigger.

It was twisted irony. Sasha's use of her husband's life insurance to fund his murder is how Richard got the idea of killing for profit. And she became his first victim, though he had a more important motive. Sasha had her own life insurance policy, and she made Suzanne Dixon her beneficiary. However, Henkel said self-preservation was his reason for killing Sasha.

"I know all about the insurance policy, but that wasn't the motive," he told investigators. "I had heard that Sasha was telling people that she had contracted out the thing [to kill Glenn Scott]. Now, I didn't know who she had told, it just come to me through the grapevine. So, I didn't know how much Sasha knew.

She didn't know through me, certainly, that I was involved. She had talked to this other guy several times, and I didn't know if she put two and two together."

Likewise, Henkel's accomplice in Glenn Scott's murder was getting concerned. Both contract killers suspected Sasha might have, as Henkel would sometimes say, "diarrhea of the mouth."

"I heard that Sasha said she was quitting and going to Florida with some guy," Henkel told detectives. "She was leaving because her and Joe [presumably Joey DeMarco] had had a real big row about something. I found out later she was only supposed to be going on vacation. I went and talked to [the person who went with me to kill Glenn Scott]. He asked me, could I be sure that Sasha wasn't talking to anyone about Scotty's murder. I told him no. So, because Joe was having a beef with her anyhow, we decided to send a package ... We did it at the Gemini to make authorities think it was a part of the massage parlor violence going on."

Henkel said he wore a disguise when he gave a cabbie twenty dollars to deliver the gift-wrapped bomb. He heard about the explosion later while he was Christmas shopping with his son and Suzanne.

"We were shopping at a mall and we passed a TV store and they had the news on. Suzanne saw the bombing coverage at the Gemini and said we need to get home. We went home and she was hit hard by Sasha's death. It was the first time I saw Suzanne cry. I went into Sasha's room and cleaned it up. I found her book with all her tricks in it and destroyed it. I didn't think the police needed to bother her clients.

"A day or two after Sasha died, two city detectives came to our apartment. I answered the door with the chain still attached. They told me a cab driver identified me. I asked them if they had a warrant. They said no, I said goodbye and shut the door."

Longtime Henkel associate Allan Frendzel revealed plots to kill Sasha Scott and Suzanne Dixon before the women were murdered. He said Henkel offered him $5,000 to murder Scott.

"He made the remark several times—that he'd like to get rid of her," Frendzel testified.

Billy Rethage, another Henkel associate, said, "Glenn Scott's insurance was supposed to go to Sasha. Her insurance was supposed to go to Henkel's fiancée, Suzanne Dixon. And Henkel was supposed to get all the money and be rich. That came out of Mr. Henkel's mouth to me. As this went on, Richard would wind up with all the money from life insurance cases. This was the big way to make money, the easy way. He didn't say how much, but he said as it goes on, it's going to be bigger."

To discourage life insurance benefit collection as a motive or incentive for murder, most US states and many countries have "slayer statutes" on the books. The laws vary but generally prevent persons involved in or suspected of intentional murder from inheriting money or property from their victims or otherwise benefitting from their crimes. Some jurisdictions have expanded their slayer rules to apply to cases of abuse or financial exploitation.

Debbie Gentile

Richard Henkel pleaded guilty to arranging Debbie Gentile's murder. Still, in later years, he said he was "shocked" that she told a psychologist she was afraid she would be murdered by her boss.

"She made that all up," he said and added that Debbie moved to California before he ever thought about harming her.

Jack Siggson testified that Richard admitted to having Debbie Gentile murdered but told him he had an alibi for the actual slaying. Siggson told police he suspected that two members of Henkel's crew were Debbie's actual killers because "they seem to do a lot of his dirty work for him." Neither Henkel nor any other suspect was tied forensically to Debbie Gentile's murder scene.

On the day that Debbie was on a plane to Pittsburgh, Henkel spent time with an insurance agent. In an interview with a newspaper reporter, and in a telling example of his mindset, he reportedly laughed at the irony of purchasing a $100,000 life insurance policy on himself while Gentile was heading toward her death.

In the book *Pittsburgh Characters*, author Paul Maryniak aptly summed up the tragedy that befell Debbie. "She was the perfect patsy for a narcissist who needed no degree in psychology to persuade cons to take the blame for his crimes, and, as Gentile's own murder demonstrated, even to persuade women to take out life insurance on themselves for him."

CHAPTER 22

In January 1985, the Pennsylvania State Superior Court ruled on Judge Cappy's dismissal of the bomb kidnap plot charges. Appeals judges decided that the conspiracy was within the applicable statute of limitations and Henkel, Gary Small, Henry Ford and Roy Travis had to stand trial. Small appealed to the Supreme Court of Pennsylvania. Before they heard the case, District Attorney Bob Colville dropped the charges after "reevaluating the strength of the case."

Gary Small appealed his termination from the police force to the Edgewood Civil Service Commission. He wanted reinstatement and full back pay. Attorney Paul Boas filed the paperwork, but in the meantime, his client moved to Japan. In 1987, Small obtained employment as a sports director for US armed forces in Okinawa.

Edgewood officials wanted a lawyer to unravel, review, and present the evidence to their Civil Service Commission to justify Small's termination. They tapped James Ross, a former US attorney, who had experience prosecuting organized crime and narcotics cases. Ross was assisted by Allegheny County Detective Bob Payne and US Alcohol, Tobacco, and Firearms Agent Bill Petraitis, a formidable combination well-versed in all things

Richard Henkel. Security was heavy for the two key witnesses they presented—Jack Siggson and Charles Kellington.

In an opening statement, James Ross said he would try to prove that Small's activities were so egregious that it rose to the level of criminal conduct.

Paul Boas said Small was a victim of circumstances. He said his client neither played a part in the bomb kidnap conspiracy nor knew Henkel possessed a firearm. "He was cleared of both charges," Boas said.

Bob Payne testified that Henkel told detectives Gary Small did not participate in any of the murders to which he had confessed. Boas emphasized Henkel's manipulative nature. He described him as a pathological liar who deceived many people, including Small.

In a closing statement, James Ross said, "There is no way you can let this man back on the police force."

In the end, the civil service commissioners concurred. They agreed with the borough's allegations that Small's association with Richard Henkel constituted conduct unbecoming of an officer. And when the former cop took no action to stop the bomb kidnap conspiracy and failed to report a crime when Henkel reportedly took a gun from his safe, it was neglect of duty. Accordingly, the commission upheld the termination. Gary Small would remain in Japan as a military sports director. But he had a side gig. And it wasn't in plumbing.

In December 1992, Small had a nineteen-gallon electric water heater shipped to himself from Pittsburgh. Japanese customs officials at Naha Airport looked inside the unit and discovered two rifles, eight semiautomatic pistols, and four hundred rounds of ammunition. When Small arrived to retrieve the water heater, he was arrested. Authorities suspected him of selling weapons to the Yakuza, a Japanese organized crime group. Small was eventually indicted for violating Japan's weapons and customs laws. Each of the counts was punishable by a prison term exceeding one year. In April 1994, a three-judge court in Naha convicted Small on all counts. They sentenced him to five years in prison and gave him credit for the ten months he had been jailed. He was released on parole in November 1996, returned to the Pittsburgh area, and eventually took a job at a junkyard.

In June 1998, a month after his Japanese parole ended, Small visited sporting goods store in Westmoreland County to purchase a handgun. He filled out the federal application; it had numerous questions including one of note.

Have you ever been convicted in any court of a crime for which the judge could have imprisoned you for more than one year?

Small answered no.

It took about eight months for the paperwork to catch up. In 1999, a federal grand jury indicted Small for unlawfully possessing a firearm. In 2002, he entered a conditional plea of guilty to possession of a firearm by a felon. US District Judge Robert Cindrich sentenced Small to eight months in federal prison and three years of supervised release. He was permitted to remain free, pending an appeal, during which Paul Boas argued that Congress did not intend to include foreign convictions when it wrote the gun law.

Judge Cindrich rejected the appeal, so Small took his argument to the US Third Circuit Court of Appeals. They affirmed Cindrich's ruling, saying that the Japanese conviction was "sufficiently consistent with our concepts of fundamental fairness . . ."

Small had one option. Bolstered by the confidence of his lawyer, Paul Boas, he petitioned the United States Supreme Court to consider the case.

Boas wrote, "It would make no sense that Congress intended to give someone less protection when his conviction was obtained in Iraq, Afghanistan or some foreign jurisdiction as opposed to a court in the United States . . . If you start using foreign convictions, you run the risk of every little two-bit military dictatorship with a case against a political prisoner being used as the basis for a conviction."

The Supreme Court found the issue of national significance and decided to hear the case. In late 2004, Paul Boas went to Washington. He said Small, fifty-eight by now, was too sick to attend due to numerous ailments from his military service. These included a back injury, post-traumatic stress disorder, and exposure to agent orange—the herbicide used by the US military to clear vegetation during the Vietnam War.

In 2005, the Supreme Court ruled that "any court" meant any American court. The high court overturned Small's firearms conviction. Owing to his US Supreme Court victory, the former cop was never convicted of a crime in the US.

Former homicide cop Bob Payne worked the Henkel case for five years. He was familiar with the details surrounding the allegations against Gary Small.

"I lived it. It was an odyssey," said Payne. "Gary Small had a great ability to mislead people. He was an intelligent man. He knew how to play the system . . . We suspected Small was actually involved with Henkel in some of these killings. Certainly our records supported that. I grew to dislike what Gary stood for . . . He's a black eye to law enforcement."

Neither Small nor any of Henkel's other associates were indicted in connection with any murders to which Henkel admitted or in which authorities believe he was involved.

Gary Small, now seventy-six, has remained silent and has not spoken directly to reporters. Back in 1980, when he was suspended as a police officer, he simply told the Edgewood mayor that a "number of false allegations" had been made against him.

CHAPTER 23

Shortly after Richard Henkel was sentenced to life in prison, *Post-Gazette* reporter Carole Patton interviewed him at length. She found he could be charming and humorous then speak calmly and candidly about shooting someone in the head. Henkel maintained that he never took a life indiscriminately.

"I don't think you ever decide that it's okay to kill people," he said. " I don't think it's okay to kill people now. I didn't wake up one morning and decide that it was all right to kill someone. Everyone that died, there was a reason for it. There was fear that I thought they would kill me, or necessity. And after the killings, I didn't really have feelings about it one way or another."

Henkel expressed regret over the collateral injuries from the blast that killed Joann Scott. Though any sincerity seemed diluted by a contradiction of his knowledge about explosives.

"I didn't know that anyone else was going to get hurt. Bombs are indiscriminate—I knew that. I felt kind of bad about [the four injured people]. I had no feeling about [Sasha]."

As a result of the fine law enforcement work in the Gentile murder investigation, Richard admitted to five murders and was suspected by police of involvement in at least four others—Suzanne Dixon, Joseph DeMarco, Laurence Windsor, and James Barone. To be clear, Richard Henkel was never indicted for either of the following murders, and investigators had additional suspects.

Suzanne Dixon

An ex-convict quoted Henkel talking about Suzanne Dixon and saying, "The bitch is getting to know too much. She has to go but not until I get two hundred thousand dollars' worth of insurance."

Billy Rethage, the Henkel associate who wanted to "make amends with God," said Henkel told him he planted a watch in Dixon's trunk to pin the murder on Henry Ford."

Henkel insisted he was in San Diego when Suzanne was murdered and therefore could not have put Ford's watch in Dixon's car, nor could he have killed Suzanne.

Joseph DeMarco

Jack Siggson said Henkel told him there was a narcotics deal in which Joey DeMarco was cheated. Henkel attended a meeting in which several people were "leaned on" to repay the Mafia associate.

"There were a great deal of bad feelings," Siggson said. "Dick thought this was also directed toward him since he was at the meeting with DeMarco."

"Yes, I was a friend of Joe DeMarco," Henkel said years later. "From what I learned from people who knew about things, Joe and a black associate went to Youngstown and got a kilo of pure cocaine on credit from a mob guy that Joey DeRose introduced him to. The black guy cut half of the coke like five times making it unsellable. Then, he was supposedly arrested with five ounces of the cocaine. He got released on a low bond. Joe had me test the coke that was cut and I told him it was unsellable. But when I tested the other half, it was not pure. It had been cut, too, with a baby laxative. Joe was pissed, called Joey DeRose and said he was going to kill the people in Youngstown who sold him the stuff. So, I think that is why Joe DeMarco died.

Two days after Joey DeMarco went missing, his brother called Henkel. They met at the old Hotel Carlton House in downtown Pittsburgh.

"He asked me if I knew a Joey Rose," Henkel said." I said no. I knew he meant Joey DeRose, but he said Joey Rose. He was the same brother who said I was not welcome at Joey D's funeral."

Jack Siggson felt Richard was probably responsible for DeMarco's death. "I told him if he keeps having all these bodies show up around him, sooner or later he's going to wind up with a charge of murder and one that won't be so easy to get out of," Siggson stated. "You can only push your luck so much and can't keep trying to rub people's faces in it, mainly the authorities, because they can make a lot of mistakes, all you have to make is one."

Siggson said that when he asked Richard Henkel about DeMarco's murder, he "told me a run-around story and smiled."

Laurence Windsor

In 1983, as part of District Attorney Kim Riester's strategy in the Gentile murder trial, three witnesses made statements about their conversations with Henkel. Billy Rethage claimed Henkel killed a fellow bank robber by repeatedly striking him with a hammer and then burying his body in lime. Richard knew who Rethage's source was.

"It was a dear friend of mine that told Billy he helped me bury a guy after I killed him with a sledgehammer," Henkel said years later.

The reported motive was for Henkel to take his share of the loot. Another witness recalled Henkel talking about burying cadavers in lime to hasten decomposition. Investigators matched the witness's details with documented specifics of a 1969 bank heist and believed the victim was Laurence Windsor.

One of the witnesses said Henkel joked about the FBI thinking Windsor was in England.

James Barone

According to a *Post-Gazette* story, police also linked Henkel to the apparent murder of James Barone. He was arrested with Henkel in 1969 for bank burglary. Not long after, he was implicated in a large counterfeiting operation and consequently became a federal informant. Federal authorities believe Barone was slain in 1970. However, his body was never found.

* * *

Richard Henkel told Jack Siggson he murdered twenty-eight people.

"If he says he killed twenty-eight people, I believe him," said Henkel's former attorney, Paul Gettleman.

Are there nineteen more beyond the five known and four suspected victims? If so, who are they? Where are the bodies? Or was Henkel aggrandizing in order to bolster his reputation?

While his number of claimed victims may be in doubt, it's certain that Richard Henkel's name struck anxiety in Pennsylvania and Ohio crime circles. Even top mob bosses feared him. Paul Maryniak reported that an informant told cops that either Pittsburgh Mafia don John LaRocca or his lieutenant Kelly Mannarino once asked the killer what it would cost to keep him away from them. Many years later, Henkel would deny the claim.

Journalist Carole Patton asked Henkel whether he regretted the way his life turned out.

"You don't know if you regret what you did or regret that you got caught," he said. "It becomes mirrored, and you don't know which is which."

For inmates, the passing of time often brings remorse for crimes and regret over a life poorly lived. Richard Henkel has been incarcerated for forty-two years. Not long after he was sentenced to life in prison, he said, "I'll spend the rest of my life thinking about going home."

Perhaps, at age eighty-three, "home" has taken on a different connotation.

Back in 1984, Richard Henkel suggested that someday he might reveal secrets but will not implicate associates. As his clock ticks down, will there be any clearing of conscience or cleansing of soul before it's too late? Will he bring closure to the family members of his victims? I asked him.

CHAPTER 24

Richard Henkel initially declined my 2021 request to answer questions about his past for *There's More Bodies Out There*. The eighty-three-year-old said he wanted to take his memories to the grave and not hurt any of his former associates or their families, even indirectly. I asked if I could write to him again in six months to let him know how the book was coming. He said that would be okay. My persistence paid off.

Beginning with my second attempt, in late 2021, Richard Henkel corresponded with me via handwritten letters, for ten months, prior to completion of this book. By that time, he had been incarcerated for almost forty-two years. He was candid about his personal history and in his claims of betrayal by former associates, emphasizing that he never talked to anyone about murders he committed.

In one of my first questions, I asked Henkel what led him into a life of crime. He said he was never in trouble until he committed his first bank robbery at age twenty-three. I asked him what went wrong.

"There was no abuse or trauma that led me astray. I had a loving family. I was drinking when it happened. I started drinking in the military. When I did most crimes, I did not drink. It was better to be sober. I quit drinking when I was twenty-eight."

After the exchange of several letters, I started asking Henkel about some of the murders to which he admitted committing or in which his involvement was suspected. I was as direct as I could be knowing he could simply stop replying to my questions if I pushed too hard.

Some Youngstown area investigators suspected Richard of involvement in mob related murders in Youngstown, Ohio in the late 1970s. In particular were those believed committed by Joe DeRose, the Cleveland Mafia enforcer in Ohio's Mahoning Valley. I asked Henkel about DeRose's ambitions and if he worked with him on occasion.

"I never heard Joey DeRose say he wanted to be a mob boss in Youngstown. I think he was really sick over his friend of many years who betrayed him. All I know is the guy ran a bingo game for Joey Naples. This guy told Naples that Joey and I were going to kill him. I don't know if he made this up or if Joey DeRose told him. But I had no idea that Naples wanted me dead. I believe [this betrayal is] why Joey wanted to kill the bingo guy first even though it was Naples who put the contract on him. Yes, I worked with Joey DeRose a couple of times."

I asked Henkel about the murder of his pregnant fiancée. He maintained, as he always has, that he was in San Diego, California when Suzanne Dixon was viciously killed. He also said her pregnancy was tubal and thus nonviable. He seemed angry at my inquiry.

"I would never hurt my child!!!"

When I referenced a source that claimed Suzanne worked at Gemini Spa, Henkel took exception.

"Let us get this straight," he said. "Suzanne never, never worked at Gemini Spa or any other spa. She was not a prostitute. So whoever wrote that is a f - - - - - - liar. God, what lies people tell on the dead. When I read that in your letter, I was really pissed."

Richard told me he did not actually kill Debbie Gentile. He had an alibi that developed by accident when his nephew was staying with him overnight—the same night Gentile was brutally murdered at the airport hotel. Henkel's ex-wife called unexpectedly and said she had to pick up her parents at the airport. She wanted Henkel to watch their son, who was twelve years old.

"Naturally, I said yes," Henkel said. "I love my son. She dropped him off and left. She called me three times saying the plane had not come in yet. I took my son and nephew to get pizza. I over-tipped as usual. My ex didn't get to my place until midnight. By then, my son was asleep. I carried him out to car and put him in backseat with his grandparents, then I went in the house to sleep."

The following day was when Henkel's nephew caught his uncle's wrath for allowing Detectives Payne and Fitzgerald to enter the house and use the telephone.

Occasionally, Henkel used humor. When I recently asked him if he needed funds for postage, he wrote, "No, thank you. But I could use a self-flying helicopter if you have a spare handy." [smiley face]

When I asked where he would go in a helicopter, he wrote, "At my age, probably to a hospital."

I questioned Henkel regarding Siggson's statement about almost being murdered. Henkel denied that was the plan.

"I was worried because Jack refused to follow my advice and my attorney's advice. But I did not lure him to Mike Mullen's house to kill him. Jack wanted to be close to town, that's all. And if I wanted to kill Jack at that time, his friend wouldn't have stopped me, for I would have just had to dig a bigger grave. And Jack's wife would have been with Jack."

Richard made a point to say he would not have killed Jack Siggson's small child.

Henkel said that after he and Siggson and his friend left Mullen's house, they went over to his Ross Township apartment. Then, he, Jack, and his friend went to collect money owed to Jack for gold coins.

If Henkel had no intention of killing Jack Siggson during the uncomfortable meeting at Mullen's house, the next day was a different story.

"Jack came to my apartment and said he wanted thirty thousand dollars. I knew then he was going to rat, but his friend was parked nearby. And I could not find him in California because he moved out of his house."

Henkel responded sparsely to my questions about his relationship with Gary Small. He blamed the police chief for Small being fired.

"When Gary suggested that we share an apartment, he said he needed to get permission from his chief. He got oral permission. Later the chief lied and said Gary never requested permission. He should have got it in writing."

In one letter, Henkel seemed eager to tell me about a conspiracy of false statements against him from convicted burglar Jackie Boyd and his friend Billy Rethage. Rethage testified that Henkel told him about murders he committed. However, Henkel said he never told anyone about any murders he committed. Instead, he suggested that Rethage's details came from grand jury notes from the kidnap murder conspiracy investigation.

"Because the grand jury had so much material, and usually defendants are not entitled to it till trial, I suggested to my attorney that my homicide trial would have to be stopped for us to review it. The district attorney objected, but the judge ruled in our favor. When I learned I was being transferred from county jail to Western Pen for security reasons, I left my copy with Junior Kripplebauer."

Kripplebauer, the notorious burglar, was serving time for interstate transportation of stolen goods when he was charged for participating in the bomb kidnap plot. He was brought to Pittsburgh and held at Allegheny County Jail where Henkel was held. According to Henkel, Kripplebauer wanted to read the notes because his girlfriend had made an appearance at the grand jury.

"So, like a dummy, I left the notes with Junior," Richard said. "I instructed him not to share them with anyone, especially Jackie Boyd, since they had become friendly on the tier, and to give them to Henry Ford when he was done with them. Against my instructions, Junior let Jackie Boyd read the grand jury notes about homicides. Apparently, Jackie made his own notes and gave them to Billy to use in his statement."

The bomb kidnap conspiracy charge against Kripplebauer was eventually dropped because prosecutors failed to bring him to trial promptly.

When I told Henkel that I had requested and received a copy of his US Air Force military discharge paperwork, he seemed disappointed and or angry.

"Why did you request my paperwork? Didn't you believe me when I told you I was in the Air Force? I have not lied to you once! I may not have answered all of your questions and left out some last names, but I have not lied. I was happy to give you factual information because your sources had some serious things wrong about Henry, Suzanne. Gary, and of course, me. Debbie, too."

When I asked Henkel how he passes the time, he said he reads and plays chess. He plays cards sometimes but has lost interest after forty-two years. At age eighty-four, he is surprisingly active. In addition to walking, he lifts weights and plays pickleball.

I was curious whether Richard Henkel embraced religion. He threw me a curve when he said he regularly attended certain religious celebrations.

"I still have not turned to religion and never will unless he blows down these walls. [smiley face]. I attend religious holiday celebrations for the food and sweets."

Henkel provided me with a couple of "tidbits," as he referred to them. In one he spoke of a large payroll holdup plan that Joey DeMarco brought to him. The mob associate and nightclub operator wanted Henkel to bring Charles Kellington with him. Henkel did not trust the drug gang enforcer.

"I told Joey I would take Chuckie on the job and then bury him. He said no, so the score never happened."

Henkel provided me with an answer about the mystery of the gas masks that were found in the vacant office for his jewelry business. Richard did not select the Clark Building for its bustling Golden Triangle location. Rather, he was far more interested in the dozens of other jewelry stores and gem dealers that called the twenty-three-floor "jewelry district" building home—specifically, a large jewelry company on the fourteenth and fifteenth floors. Henkel obtained their property inventory.

"It showed five million dollars' worth of gemstones and jewelry. Of course, some of that would have been sold. We disabled the alarm, but the business had another security system on the fifteenth floor. The police came and brought a dog. We ran up to my office on the twenty-second floor. The masks were there in case we needed them [for police tear gas]," Henkel said. "But the dog went past my office, the police eventually left, and we left in the morning."

In a disturbing revelation, Henkel claimed that the former Western Pen corrections officer who was convicted of providing the guns he used to hold hostages for five days was actually innocent of that charge. He explained that he paid a prison employee to receive a pair of shoes, in which the guns were hidden, from Henkel's outside conspirator, and wear them into the prison. It was April, and there was still snow on the ground. Richard had his accomplice put Totes (rubber rain boots) on the shoes to better conceal the weapons before giving them to the prison employee.

"Poor Roy Layne. He was innocent," Richard said. "The [guilty] guy wasn't even a CO. He was a staff member. The revolvers were 5-shot, but I only had four bullets put in each gun because I didn't want the guy to hit his heel hard and have one gun go off. He had no idea that the shoes had guns in them. He thought he was smuggling in hashish. I paid him two hundred dollars. When we switched shoes, he asked if he could keep the Totes, and I said yes. Those guns were never out of the shoes until the hostage situation."

In one letter, I asked Richard his thoughts on why Suzanne Dixon and Debbie Gentile were so brutally murdered.

"I cannot speak of Suzanne's murder, but it makes me sick to my stomach. Why he [the unnamed killer] did Debbie like that, I never asked. But I did tell him it was stupid and careless."

I suggested to Henkel that the police or newspaper reporters exaggerated the number of murders in which he was involved. I told him I believed it was twelve or fewer.

"No cops or reporters exaggerated the numbers. You underestimated, but I'm not getting into numbers, for who cares. I did offer to give county detectives more bodies, but I wanted immunity from prosecution. And they got no information from me to arrest anyone.

"There are some people I wish I did not kill or was in conspiracy to kill. But I did what I did. Not proud of it."

Henkel had previously mentioned using money to benefit his family. In one of my letters, I asked him about specifics. He focused on his mother telling me that he bought her a red fox fur coat and would take her to wrestling matches.

"She enjoyed wresting and loved to yell at the cheaters and the referees," he said. "I took her to dinner, movies, plays, and on vacations. I bought her a new television and a sewing machine. But all sons do this if they love their mother."

In one of my last letters, I pushed Henkel for information about the claim he used a hammer to kill a man believed to be Laurence Windsor.

"I will say this, you don't give up trying to get me to admit to a homicide," he said. "I know nothing about a hammer victim, as that's a homicide I've never been arrested, indicted, charged with. But I can assure you that I did not want his half of the bank robbery, as he got his half."

Finally, I referenced Richard Henkel's 1984 comment to a newspaper reporter about someday providing details about unsolved murders.

"No. I will never help to solve homicides," he said. "Those crimes will go to the grave with me. And what do I have to lose? Some carry the death sentence, though I would die of natural causes before the chair. And if I would even hint at solving homicides, some slick detective would probably say, 'I theorize you may have did this with this person or that person,' just like some author trying to get information that could hurt people. You know what I mean."

Dear Reader,

I hope that you enjoyed this book which was the culmination of four years of research and writing. Reader reviews are vital for authors. Please consider leaving an honest review at your favorite online book blog, book retailer, or social networking site. Thank you!

Cordially yours,

Rick Porrello

SOURCES

CORRESPONDENCE
Personal correspondence with Richard E. Henkel 2021-2022

NEWSPAPERS
Pittsburgh Press
Pittsburgh Post-Gazette
Intelligencer Journal (Lancaster)
The Times-Tribune (Scranton)
The Philadelphia Inquirer

GOVERNMENT DOCUMENTS
Allegheny County, PA Police Department, Commonwealth of Pennsylvania vs. Richard Henkel, Homicide investigations of Deborah Gentile, Glenn Scott, Joann Scott, Andrew Russman and Bruce Agnew, 1980-1984. Limited access.

Allegheny County, PA Coroner's Office, Reports of death: Deborah Gentile and Joann Scott.

Commonwealth of Pennsylvania, Appellant, v. Richard HENKEL; Superior Court of Pennsylvania; Argued January 11, 1982; Filed November 15, 1982.

Pennsylvania Crime Commission, A Decade of Organized Crime 1980 Report, Commonwealth of Pennsylvania, Sep. 1980.

U.S. Federal Bureau of Investigation, Memo dated June 21, 1979, from the Philadelphia SAC to the Pittsburgh SAC regarding Thomas Frederick Seher.

U.S. Supreme Court, No. 03-750, "Gary Small, Petitioner v. US, Apr. 26, 2005, via www.law.cornell.edu, accessed Apr. 20, 2022

U.S. Senate, Committee on Governmental Affairs. Permanent Subcommittee on Investigations Ninety-eighth Congress, Second Session. Profile of Organized Crime, Great Lakes Region : Hearings Before the Permanent Subcommittee on Investigations of the Committee on Governmental Affairs, January 25, 26, 31, and February 1, 1984.

TELEVISION ARCHIVES
Pittsburgh Action 4 News

BOOKS

Aurand, Martin. *The Spectator and the Topographical City.* University of Pittsburgh Press, Pittsburgh, PA, 2014.

Hornblum, Allen M. *Confessions of a Second Story Man – Junior Kripplebauer and the K&A Gang.* Barricade Books, Inc. Fort Lee, NJ, 2006.

Maryniak, Paul, *Pittsburgh Characters*, ed. Roy McHugh, "Serial Killing for Profit," Iconoclast Press, Greensburg, PA, 1991.

Porrello, Rick. *Superthief – A Master Burglar, the Mafia, and the Biggest Bank Heist in US History.* Next Hat Press. Cleveland, OH, 2006.

Schwartz, Jeffrey H., *What the Bones Tell Us*, The University of Arizona Press, Tucson, AZ, 1993.

ONLINE ARTICLES

Scott Burnstein, "The Flames of Discontent in Youngstown," www.gangsterreport.com, accessed Apr. 20. 2022.

ENDNOTES

Chapter 1

p. 05 About the Henkel family:
   US Census, 1930, Westmoreland County, PA. Accessed Nov. 11, 2021.
   www.familysearch.org.
   County marriage records, West Virginia, 1776-1971. Accessed Nov. 15,
   2021. www.familysearch.org.
   "What 3-Year Old 'Driver' Did To Another Car," *The Pittsburgh Press*,
   May 20, 1941.

p. 07 Good Conduct Medal:
   www.afpc.af.mil/Fact-Sheets/Display/Article/421952/air-force-good-
   conduct-medal/. Accessed June 24, 2022.

p. 07 Death of Frank Henkel:
   Death notice, Frank B. Henkel. *Pittsburgh Press*, Mar. 10, 1963.

Chapter 2

pp. 10-11 Bank robberies and burglaries:
   The Pittsburgh Press, Sep. 15, 1960.
   The Pittsburgh Press, April 21, 1969.
   Pittsburgh Post-Gazette, April 22, 1969.
   Pittsburgh Post-Gazette, June 19, 1969.

p. 12 "It was apparent to me"
   Jim Gallagher and J. Kenneth Evans, "Hostage-taker Portrayed as Jekyll
   and Hyde," *Pittsburgh Post-Gazette*, April 16, 1983.

p. 13 sentenced to serve time concurrently: Author conjecture

Chapter 3

p. 15 Henkel joined the Jaycees:
   Maryniak, Paul, *Pittsburgh Characters*. (Roy McHugh) Greensburg, PA,
   Iconoclast Press, 1991.

p. 15 investors like Lee took an interest:

Other reputed investors in the Pittsburgh sex trade included Martin Berger, Stephen Israeloff, and Harry Jessup. .
Stolberg, Mary, "DeLucia Trial Skirts In-Depth View of Rub Racket," *The Pittsburgh Press*, Nov. 17, 1980. And *Pittsburgh Post-Gazette*, Feb. 14, 1975.

p. 16 "I just had to shoot him"
Jack Grochot, "At Smut Shop, Ironworker Wears Different Hat," *Pittsburgh Press*, Apr. 23, 1972

p. 16 linked by family ties:
State and local lawmen who investigated the massage parlor racket uncovered specific connections to the Pittsburgh mob. They believed that Antonio Ripepi was the Pitt mob's money man and thus controlled the cash flow generated by much of the city's massage parlor prostitution. His son-in-law, John Bazzano, Jr., reportedly served as a street collector. "Cosa Nostra Family Linked to Rub Racket," *Pittsburgh Post-Gazette*, Jan. 31, 1978.

p. 17 "If you check the background," *Pittsburgh Post-Gazette*, Dec. 29, 1977.

Chapter 4

p. 20 "After all" *Pittsburgh Post-Gazette*, Jan. 31, 1978.

p. 21 "objectionable from the standpoint of consumer protection"
"Legitimate Masseurs Map Battle," *The Pittsburgh Press*, Feb. 18, 1973.

p. 21 A Pittsburgh Press editorial weighed in: *The Pittsburgh Press*, Feb. 26, 1973.

p. 21 "They are ruining the reputation," *The Pittsburgh Press*, Feb. 18, 1973.

p. 22 "I can't really see anything illegitimate," Hritz, "DePasquale"

p. 22 It obviously represented a hefty investment:
Robert Voelker, "When Is a Massage Not Just a Massage," *Pittsburgh Post-Gazette*, Dec. 7, 1972

p. 22 "good for the city"
Thomas M. Hritz, "DePasquale Is Rubbed Right Way," *Pittsburgh Post-Gazette*, Dec. 7, 1972

p. 23 "The only thing going on"
"Massage Parlors Called Convention Lure," *Pittsburgh Post-Gazette*, Mar. 17, 1976.

Chapter 5

p. 27 Roy Travis
Stan Shillington, "Police Seize Yacht After Flyer Held in U.S; Huge Drug Ring Believed Found," *The Sunday Sun* (Vancouver), Feb. 13, 1965.
"Seventeen Years for Canada Pilot," *The Times* (San Mateo, CA), May 3, 1965.

p. 28 "I'm not trying to assign blame," *Pittsburgh Post-Gazette*, Jan. 3, 1975.

p 31 Jack Siggson served time for shooting and killing a man: This was Albert Casanova.
"Two Men Sentenced for May Murder," *Courier-Post*, (Camden) Dec. 18, 1968.
p. 31 "Jack the Jew," Commonwealth vs. Richard Henkel investigations
p. 32 "bus stop" Commonwealth v. Henkel investigations
p. 32 The owner was said to be Antonio Ripepi: Maryniak, *Pittsburgh Characters*
p. 32-33 DeMarco and Kellington
Paul Maryniak, "Officials See Henkel Cunning in Plea Bargain," *The Pittsburgh Press*, Jan. 15, 1984.
"Monster Lives Up to His Nickname" *The Pittsburgh Press*, Jan. 29, 1982.

Chapter 6
p. 35 "You look like a Russian princess," Interview with anonymous, March 2022
p. 36 She agreed with the plan: Author conjecture
p. 36 Franco Harris and several of his Pittsburgh Steelers teammates:
Connie Giel, "Did Youth Horse Camp Take County for Ride," *Pittsburgh Press*, April 25, 1977
p. 36 "When DeMarco saw her" Commonwealth v. Henkel investigations
p. 38 Henkel pulled up the hilly entrance: Commonwealth v. Henkel investigations.
p. 38 "Wait a minute," Commonwealth v. Henkel investigations

Chapter 7
p. 39 The teacher only lasted a year: Interview with anonymous.
p. 39 "marvelous with their children"
"Runaway Milwaukee Girl is Pittsburgh Bombing Victim," *The Capital Times*, Dec. 28, 1977.
p. 40 "Joann spent a lot of time there," Interview with anonymous, March 2022
p. 41 Danny Harris, better known as Danilo "Chico" Artez:
Nick Coleman and Doug Stone, Artez Calls Charges Against Him Harassing, *Star Tribune*, Jan. 28, 1979.
p. 41 "Chico made us light his cigarettes"
Doug Stone, "Artez's Main Lady: Going to Prison but Feeling Free, *Star Tribune*, June 29, 1979.
p. 42 two prostitutes who were charged:
They were Jacqueline Hayes Hatch, killed in Memphis, TN, and Sharon K. Davis, murdered in New York City.
Don Jensen, "The Jacqueline Hayes Hatch Murder Story," *Kenosha News*, Feb. 14, 1974.
p. 42 Scotty was standing over her: Commonwealth v. Henkel investigations.
p. 43 "Scotty would call over" Commonwealth v. Henkel investigations.

p. 43 At the Court Lounge, she informed a friend: Author conjecture.
p. 44 Dick sensed Glenn was suspicious:
Author conjecture based on Commonwealth v. Henkel investigations.
p. 44 "Dick Henkel was the wrong guy" Commonwealth v. Henkel investigations.
p. 44 In September 1975, Sasha and Sue Dixon scheduled:
Paul Maryniak, "Airport Slay Trial Takes a New Twist," *The Pittsburgh Press*, Apr. 19, 1981.
p. 44 "What should I do?" Commonwealth v. Henkel investigations.

Chapter 8
pp. 45-46 Chatzispiros bombing:
"Special delivery bomb kills father," *The Vancouver Sun*, Oct. 6, 1975.
"Killer Bomb Tagged Literature," *The Province* (Vancouver), Oct. 7, 1975
p. 46 in a cabin in Canonsburg:
Hornblum, Allen M. *Confessions of a Second Story Man – Junior Kripplebauer and the K&A Gang*. Barricade Books, Inc. Fort Lee, NJ, 2006
p. 46 it catered to wealthy clients: Hornblum, *Confessions*
p. 48 and a female massage parlor employee: This was Debbie Dremsek
"Principal Characters in Massage Parlor Drama," *Pittsburgh Post-Gazette*, Jan. 31, 1978.

Chapter 9
p. 51 "It's from Randy," Author created based on Commonwealth v. Henkel investigations.
p. 51 whooped and chuckled: Author created.
p. 51-52 bombing murder of Sasha Scott:
Alvin Rosensweet, "Porno War Sparks Mayor's Crackdown," *Pittsburgh Post-Gazette*, Dec. 24, 1977.
Joyce Gemperlein and Lorraine Macklin, "Yule Cheer Interrupted by Blast," *Pittsburgh Post-Gazette*, Dec. 24, 1977.
Connie Giel, "Hooker, Mate Pawns in War?" *The Pittsburgh Press*, Dec. 24, 1977.
p. 53 suspicious package at the residence of Nick Delucia:
William Allan, Jr., "Package at Kingpin's Home a Real 'Present'," *The Pittsburgh Press*, Dec. 24, 1977.
p. 53 A wood plank propped against: Author conjecture.
p. 54 "The bombing would have been a stupid move"
Charles Lynch, "Rub Parlors Remain Closed After Bombing," *Pittsburgh Post-Gazette*, Dec. 26, 1977.
p. 54 He suggested that someone may have directed:
Geoffrey Tomb, "City Massage Parlors Reopen as State Court Reverses Ruling," *The Pittsburgh Press*, Dec. 31, 1977
p. 56 "Gambling is a game for suckers," *Cleveland Press*, March 14, 1935.
p. 56 "They had planned to give," Commonwealth v. Henkel investigations.

Chapter 10

p. 59 Debbie Gentile was born Deborah Kelber: Unconfirmed by birth certificate

p. 59 "They just married too young"
Jim Gallagher, "Victim's Brother: Bargain is Lenient," *Pittsburgh Post-Gazette*, Jan. 12, 1984.

p. 60 Suzanne Dixon learned she was pregnant:
Charles Lynch, "Stabbed Shot Body, Vice Figure Tied," *Pittsburgh Post-Gazette*, May 29, 1978

p. 61 Jack Siggson and Henry Ford spent several days:
Linda Wilson, "Suspect in Bomb Plot Lied in Probe, Trial Told," *Pittsburgh Post-Gazette*, Mar. 24, 1982.

p. 61 and watched through a window
Eleanor Chute, "Killer Testifies in Rooney Bomb-Extortion Plot," *The Pittsburgh Press*, May 1, 1981

p. 62 Suzanne Dixon murder:
"Woman's Body Found; Vice War Tie Probed," *The Pittsburgh Press*, May 28, 1978
Charles Lynch, "Stabbed, Shot Body, Vice Figure Tied," *Pittsburgh Post-Gazette*, May 29, 1978.
Rich Gigler, "Brutal Slaying Called Message in Brutal Vice War," *The Pittsburgh Press*, May 30, 1978

p. 63 "I have life insurance"
Paul Maryniak, "Airport-Slay Suspect Linked to Unsolved Killings" *The Pittsburgh Press*, Oct. 24, 1980.

p. 64 "We never bought that story"
Paul Maryniak, "Airport Slaying Perjury Suspect Linked to '78 Killing" *The Pittsburgh Press*, Dec. 21, 1980.

p. 65 "I'm into something with persons," Gallagher, "Victim's Brother"

Chapter 11

p. 68 he was financially stretched: Author conjecture.

p. 68 "I can't help you in any way," Commonwealth vs. Henkel

p. 69 "It's a quick way to pick up a lot of money," Commonwealth vs. Henkel

p. 70 "we should fill these out," Gentile homicide file.

p. 70 Henkel directed Gentile to leave several lines blank: Author conjecture.

p. 71 It had been a long time: Author conjecture

p. 71 Debbie wrote to her mom daily: Gallagher, "Victim's Brother"

p. 71 suspicious of Siggson: Author conjecture

p. 71 "She dresses like a prostitute," Commonwealth v. Henkel investigations.

p. 73 "I know if I go back to Pittsburgh," Commonwealth v. Henkel investigations.

Chapter 12

p. 75 As a boy: Interview with Bob Payne, Aug. 2021

p. 76 "I think she was more scared," Gallagher, "Victim's Brother

p. 77 "We have no proof supporting"
"Reason for Slain Woman's Return Here Still Mystery," *Pittsburgh Post-Gazette*," May 22, 1979.

p. 78 "If you ever let someone in," Interview with Bob Payne, Aug. 2021

p. 78 a former bouncer for a Shadyside nightclub:
"Man's Disappearance Baffles Police," *The Pittsburgh Press*, Oct. 19, 1979.

p. 79 they did find a body:
"Racketeer Found Slain at Airport," *The Pittsburgh Press*, Oct. 23, 1979.

p. 79 "The DeMarco slaying is"
Fritz Huysman, "Cindrich Declares War on Organized Crime After DeMarco Slaying," *Pittsburgh Post-Gazette*, Oct. 26, 1979.

p. 79-80 a well-known drug dealer: This was Stevenson "Stoney" Bey.
Mary Stolberg, "Court Says Henkel Can't Pay for Defense, So Taxpayers Will," *The Pittsburgh Press*, Feb. 9, 1983.

p. 80 About the Clark building:
https://www.thebraggingmommy.com/the-clark-   building-in-pittsburgh-pa-and-its-rich-history-of-diamond-jewelry-stores/

p. 80 "No, no. I don't want anything done." Based on:
Paul Maryniak, "Gas-Mask Find Deepens 'Insurance Slay' Mystery," *The Pittsburgh Press*, Oct. 26, 1980.

Chapter 13
This chapter is based largely on Commonwealth v. Henkel investigations.

Chapter 14
This chapter is based largely on Commonwealth v. Henkel investigations.

Chapter 15

p. 92 "When we were in the joint," Personal interview with Phil Christopher, 2022

p. 92 "I told you that I'd get even," Personal interview with Phil Christopher, 2022

p. 94 hide out at Richard Henkel's house: Maryniak, *Pittsburgh Characters*

Chapter 16

p. 95 "If you're not with me," Commonwealth vs. Henkel investigations.

p. 95 "I'm just appalled"
Eleanor Chute, "California Court Action Stalls Rub Parlor Trial Here," *The Pittsburgh Press*," Aug. 26, 1980

p. 96 Siggson said Henkel told him Edgewood cop: Commonwealth v. Henkel investigations

p. 96 "Siggson was worried," Interview with Robert Payne, Aug. 2021

p. 98 The ATF agent was William Petraitis. The Hampton Twp. Chief was Chester Kline.

p. 98 "Richard Henkel. This is the Allegheny County Police," Author conjecture

p. 100 "It was my habit" Personal email with Paul Maryniak, May 2022

p. 101 a skilled and passionate DA:
TribLive.live.com/local/pittsburghallegheny/rosfelds-lawyer-patrick-thomassey-boasts-long-history-of-tackling-the-tough-cases. Accessed July 11, 2022.

p. 101 "He is not a witness to be believed"
Paul Maryniak, "Airport Slaying Witness Tells Tale of 'Fear'," Nov. 16, 1980.

p. 101 "I lied because I was scared"
Linda S. Wilson, "Henkel Must Stand Trial in Slaying," *Pittsburgh Post-Gazette*, Nov. 14, 1980.

p. 102 "leered and laughed" Wilson, Henkel Must Stand

p. 102 "All-American boy" and a "nice guy"
Chet Wade, "Edgewood Fires Policeman, *Pittsburgh Post-Gazette*, Jan. 31, 1981.

p. 103 violent tendencies.
Matthew Kennedy, "Threat by Slay Suspect," *The Pittsburgh Press*, Feb. 7, 1981.

p. 104 "I'm not going back to prison," Based on.
Linda S. Wilson, "Suspect Threatened Prosecutor - Officer, Pittsburgh Post-Gazette, Feb. 7, 1981.

p. 104 "*former husband had been involved in drug dealing*"
Torsten Ove, "Former Officer in New Round of Legal Woes," *Pittsburgh Post-Gazette*, Feb. 18, 2001.

p. 104 The boxes contained:
Linda S. Wilson, "Witness: I Lived in Fear After Helping Suspect Plan Murder," *Pittsburgh Post-Gazette*, Nov. 13, 1980

p. 105 "He walked up to me," Email with Paul Maryniak, May 2022.

p. 105 Joe DeRose Jr. went missing:
In 2001 Samuel "Skinny Sam" Fossesca was indicted for DeRose's murder but died before the case went to trial.

p. 105 "great reluctance and true remorse,"
Paul Maryniak, "'Slay for Insurance' Evidence Ruling Hit," *Pittsburgh Press*, Apr. 28, 1981.

Chapter 17

p. 107 "I can improve your financial situation"
Paul Maryniak, "2 Charged in County Jail Plot," *Pittsburgh Press*, Nov. 24, 1981.

p. 107 James "Sonny" Watson, an associate of Chuckie Kellington: Watson had been charged for the contract killing of Norman McGregor. Both men were in the crew of Kellington and Robert "Codfish" Bricker.

p. 108 *Dick was in court and couldn't call:* Paul Maryniak, "Probers Trace Jailbreak Try to Youngstown," *Pittsburgh Press*, Nov. 27, 1981

p. 110 *The fact that an absentee was exposed:* PA Statute 20, subsection 5701

p. 110 "I don't believe the man's alive" The agent was Lawrence Bria. Lawrence Walsh, "Wife Cites 'Peril' to Get Husband Declared Dead," *The Pittsburgh Press*, Mar. 14, 1962.

p. 111 "Under those circumstances where police" "COMMONWEALTH of Pennsylvania, Appellant, v. Richard HENKEL," *Superior Court of Pennsylvania*, Jan. 11, 1982.

p. 112 "How far did you get through school?" Paul Maryniak, "Henkel Trades Barbs with Judge," *Pittsburgh Press*, Jan. 5, 1983.

p. 113 "I knew Gary was a proud man" Mary Stolberg, "Informant on Stand in Gun Trial," *Pittsburgh Press*, Mar. 24, 1983

p. 114 "He began gesticulating wildy" Mary Stolberg, "Richard Henkel Found Guilty in Gun Trial," *Pittsburgh Press*, Mar. 26, 1983.

p. 114 "The only thing we know about Robert" Edwina Rankin, "Robert Henkel Held in Jail Escape Ploy," *Pittsburgh Press*, Apr. 22, 1983

p. 115 "You don't understand the anguish" Gallagher and Evans, "Hostage-taker"

p. 115 "common scheme" Paul Maryniak, "2 Holding Hostages Delay Hearing in 3 Killings," *Pittsburgh Press*, Apr. 14, 1983.

p. 116 "Dick was my lover" Paul Maryniak, "Henkel Bragged About Killings," *Pittsburgh Press*, Apr. 19, 1983

p. 116 "history of psychiatric illness" Susan Mannella, "Henkel Linked to Slay-for-Insurance Plot," *Pittsburgh Post-Gazette*, Apr. 19, 1983.

p. 116 a drug dealer in Florida: This was Phillip D. Hubbard.

p. 116 "insurance companies are good ways" Paul Maryniak, "Henkel Called 'Model of Rehabilitation,'" *Pittsburgh Press*, Apr. 15, 1983.

p. 116 Coviello serving life for murder: the victim was Dominick Coroniti. Tom Casey, "Coviello Loses Bid for Jail-Term Cut" *The Tribune* (Scranton), Oct. 28, 1982.

p. 117 "Smarter than the average con" Maryniak, *Pittsburgh Characters*

p. 117 Lackovic's tip about escape

Roger Stuart and William Maustellar, "Western Pen Siege Symptom of a Larger Crisis," *Pittsburgh Press*, Apr. 24, 1983.

Chapter 18

p. 120 "Don't try anything" Based on:
Dan Kohut, "Days of Terror at Western Penitentiary," *Pittsburgh Post-Gazette*, Jul. 9, 1983.

p. 120 "Mr. Mastros, please move"
Robert Baird, "'Wow, It Was Unbelievable from Then On,'", *Pittsburgh Press*, Apr. 20, 1983

p. 121 "Jesus Christ, what have we got" Baird, "Wow"

p. 122 The main negotiator:
The psychologist was Dr. Allan Pass, the counselor was Bob Pietrala, and the priest was Rev. James Salberg.

p. 123 "I thought they were going to charge"
Paul Maryniak, "Inside Hostage Story," *Pittsburgh Press*, Dec. 11, 1983.

p. 123 "We're constantly trying"
"Phone Contact Renewed in Pittsburgh Jail Siege," *Philadelphia Inquirer*, Apr. 17, 1983

p. 124 "If what they say"
Jim Gallagher and J. Kenneth Evans, "Hostage-taker Portrayed as Jekyll and Hyde," *Pittsburgh Post-Gazette*, Apr. 16, 1983

p. 125 "Ye Allegheny Sandwich Shoppe"
Robert Baird and Douglas Root, "Convicts Kept Diary of Hostage Crisis," *The Pittsburgh Press*, Apr. 21, 1983.

p. 125 He explained that the sandwich:
Author conjecture and https://en.wikipedia.org/wiki/Dagwood_sandwich

p. 125 "Rich, if I ever get out" Kohut, "Days"

p. 126 "I'm not Pavlov's dog!"
Carole Patton, "Hostage Tells of Ordeal, Thought He Was a Goner," *Pittsburgh Post-Gazette*, Apr. 21, 1983

p. 127 "I don't want any more time" Author-created based on:
John O'Brien, "Mr. Mastros, I Could Never Shoot You," *UPI*, Apr. 21, 1983.

p. 128 "If one must hang"
"Coviello Eyed Hanging Hostage," *The Times-Tribune* (Scranton), Dec. 12, 1983

Chapter 19

p. 132 "Why waste your life?" Patton, "Hostage Tells"

p. 132 "If you are the cause,"
It's Over," *Pittsburgh Post-Gazette*, Apr. 20, 1983.

p. 133 "A lot of people in Pittsburgh want Henkel dead," Patton, "Hostage Tells"

p. 133 "The warden was not present"
"No Shakedown Called at Prison Because of Cost," *The Morning Call* (Allentown), Apr. 22, 1983.

p. 134 "I would never do anything"
Susan Mannella, "Henkel: Kohut Tried to Sell Me Guns," *Pittsburgh Post-Gazette*, May 10, 1983.

p. 134 "It's nothing but a frame-up,"
Roger Stuart and Robert Baird, "Dismissed Guard Held as Supplier of Guns," *The Pittsburgh Press*, May 27, 1983.

p. 134-145 "diminished capacity"
https://www.law.cornell.edu/wex/diminished_capacity. Accessed Apr. 21, 2022.

p. 135 "I think Richard Henkel is the most manipulative person"
Susan Mannella, "Judge Puts Henkel in Mental Hospital," *Pittsburgh Post-Gazette*, Sep. 30, 1983.

p. 137-138 "Everyone worked hard all day,"
"Trial Set to Open for Dunmore Man's Partner," *The Times-Tribune* (Scranton), Jan. 11, 1984.

p. 139 "As long as he makes," Based on:
Carole Patton, "Henkel to Point Out Victims' Graves," *Pittsburgh Post-Gazette*, July 2, 1984

p. 139 "The mitigating circumstances supporting"
Douglas Root, "Henkel Pleads Guilty to Gentile Murder; Gets Life Term," *Pittsburgh Press*, Jan. 11, 1984.

p. 139 "He told me that he is happy"
Patton, "Bargain, Henkel Pleads Guilty" *Pittsburgh Post-Gazette*," Jan. 12, 1984.

p. 139 "Henkel was a 'hired killer'"
"Killer Pleads Guilty," *Intelligencer Journal* (Lancaster), Jan. 12, 1984.

p. 139 "What's the difference," Patton, "Bargain,"

p. 139 "I'm only concerned that my family"
Carole Patton, "Henkel: 'Maybe a Chance to Help My Brother,'" *Pittsburgh Post-Gazette*, Jan. 13, 1984.

p. 140 "Henkel may be demonstrating,"
Paul Maryniak, "Officials See Henkel Cunning in Plea Bargain," *The Pittsburgh Press*, Jan. 15, 1984.

Chapter 20
p. 143 "Why are you pleading guilty?"
"Others Murders Info Seen Likely," *The Times-Tribune* (Scranton), Jan. 12, 1984.

p. 143 "He's going to escape," Maryniak, "Officials See"

p. 143-144 "For a guy who controlled people," Maryniak, "Officials See"

p. 144 "I wanted to be at Henkel's execution."

THERE'S MORE BODIES OUT THERE

Jim Gallagher, "Victim's Brother: Bargain is Lenient," *Pittsburgh Post-Gazette*, Jan. 12, 1984.
p. 144 "Plus the fact that I may receive"
Douglas Root, "Diary Entry May Get Henkel New Trial," *Pittsburgh Press*, Mar. 1, 1984.
p. 146 "The information was that"
Robert Johnson and Steve Eisenberg, "Henkel back at burial site' bomb may be on 2nd body," *Pittsburgh Press*, July 20, 1984
p. 146 "I tried to explain"
Jeffrey Schwartz, *What the Bones Tell Us*, The University of Arizona Press, 1993.
p. 147 "I was scanning the ground, Schwartz, *What the Bones Tell Us*
p. 148 "As the body decomposed," Schwartz, *What the Bones Tell Us*
p. 149 "Henkel hasn't been to the area in seven years,"
Carole Patton, "Body Dig," *Pittsburgh Post-Gazette*, July 19, 1984
p. 149 "was surprised at their arrival," Johnson/Eisenberg, "Henkel Back"
p. 150 "You better lock the door"
Tim Vercellotti, "Hunt For Henkel Victims Over," *The Pittsburgh Press*, July 29, 1984
p. 150 Amidst the occasional choppy staccato: Author conjecture
p. 150 "Is that the best way," Based on: Schwartz, *What the Bones Tell Us*
p. 151 "There's more bodies out there," Interview with Bob Payne, Aug. 2021
p. 152 "We're hoping he'll cooperate"
Douglas Root, "DA Tries to Avoid Henkel Retrial," *The Pittsburgh Press*, Aug. 3, 1984
p. 152 "If he says anything about this transaction"
Jim Gallagher, "Guard Smuggled Guns to Inmates," *Pittsburgh Post-Gazette*, May 28, 1983.

Chapter 21

p. 155 numerous cops and attorneys:
Joseph Steele and David Smith of Allegheny County District Attorney's Office; John Flannigan, Terry Hediger and Ron Freeman from Pittsburgh PD; Robert Payne and Herbe Foote from Allegheny County PD; Larry Morrisey from the US Bureau of Alcohol, Tobacco and Firearms.
p. 155-161 Henkel confessions: Commonwealth v. Henkel investigations
p. 155 gone bad"
Hornblum, Allen M. *Confessions of a Second Story Man – Junior Kripplebauer and the K&A Gang*. Barricade Books, Inc. Fort Lee, NJ, 2006
p. 155 "it's your turn to dig," Patton, "Body Dig,"
p. 161 "He made the remark several times," Maryniak, "Henkel Bragged"
p. 161 "Glenn Scott's insurance was supposed to go," Mannella, "Henkel Linked"

Chapter 22

p. 163 "re-evaluating the strength of the case"
Jim Cuddy, Jr., "1981 Firing of Policeman with Dubious Ties Under Review," *The Pittsburgh Press*, Apr. 11, 1988.

p. 164 In an opening statement:
Carmen J. Lee, "Officer belonged to club where body was found," *Pittsburgh Post-Gazette*, April 15, 1984.

p. 164 "He was cleared of both charges"
"Edgewood Panel Backs Dismissal of Policeman," *The Pittsburgh Press*, May 4, 1988.

p. 164 Bob Payne testified that Henkel told detectives: Lee, "Officer Belonged"

p. 164 Boas emphasized Henkel's manipulative nature. Based on:
Susan Mannella, "Ex-officer's actions 'criminal,' commission told," *Pittsburgh Post-Gazette*, April 15, 1988.

p. 164 "There is no way"
"Ex-officer called a Jekyll-Hyde type," *Pittsburgh Post-Gazette*, April 19, 1988

p. 164 In December 1992, Small:
Small v. US, www:supreme.justia.com/cases/federal/us/544/385/ accessed Dec. 18, 2021.

p. 164 Authorities suspected him of selling
Torsten Ove, "Former Edgewood Officer Sentenced," *Pittsburgh Post-Gazette*, June 18, 2002.

p. 165 a three-judge court in Naha:
They were Chief Judge Kyoichi Miyogi, and Judges Yashiro Akiba and Kenji Tanaka. On the third day of the trial, Judge Tanaka was replaced by Judge Takeshi Ebara.

p. 165 eventually took a job at a junkyard:
Torsten Ove, "Former Officer in New Round of Legal Woes," *Pittsburgh Post-Gazette*, Feb. 18, 2001.

p. 165 "sufficiently consistent with our concepts," *US v Small*.

p. 166 Small was too sick to attend:
Chris Osher, "Top court hears Pittsburgh case," *Trib Live*, Nov. 3, 2004, archive.triblive.com/news/top-court-hears-pittsburgh-case, accessed July 26, 2021.

p. 166 "I lived it," Ove, "Former Officer"

p. 166 "A number of false allegations"
Paul Maryniak, "Slay Trial Witness Links Cop to Pistol," *The Pittsburgh Press*, Nov. 20, 1980.

Chapter 23

p. 167 "I don't think you ever"
Carole Patton, "Confessed killer's self-portrait," *Pittsburgh Post-Gazette*, Aug. 2, 1984

p. 168 "the bitch is getting to know too much" Based on: Maryniak, "Henkel Called"

p. 168 Henkel told him he planted:
Paul Maryniak, "Lover Link Henkel to Frame-up," *Pittsburgh Press*, April 21, 1983.

p. 169 "I told him if he," Commonwealth vs. Henkel

p. 170 Maryniak reported that an informant: Maryniak, "Officials See"

p. 171 "I'll spend the rest of my life" Based on: Patton, "Henkel: Maybe"

Chapter 24
This chapter is based on the author's written communication with Richard Henkel during 2022.

INDEX

Indicates mention in Endnotes only

ABOUT THE AUTHOR

Photo by Rebecca Bihun

Rick Porrello, a former police chief with mob roots, writes true crime books that attract interest from filmmakers. His first title resulted from curiosity about the murders of his grandfather and three uncles, early Mafia leaders. A later book was adapted for a documentary and the 2011 motion picture *Kill the Irishman*, currently on Netflix. He has several other projects in various stages of development.

www.rickporrello.com

Also by Rick Porrello

Bombs, Bullets, and Bribes:
The True Story of Notorious Jewish Mobster Alex Shondor Birns
(Next Hat Press, 2019)
Shondor Birns, a friend of powerful Jewish and Italian mobsters and trusted part-ner of black gambling racketeers, went toe-to-toe against relentless challengers. The cops wanted him in prison, immigration officials wanted him deported, and the IRS wanted his nightclub, car, and cash. Black gangsters wanted the old white man out of the numbers racket, and rogue underlings wanted to kill the king. *Bombs, Bullets, and Bribes* is in development for a streaming series and a documentary.

Superthief: A Master Burglar, the Mafia, and the
Biggest Bank Heist in U.S. History
(Next Hat Press, 2005)
A raw and candid accounting of burglar and Mafia associate Phil Christopher's life, with focus on the 1972 United California Bank heist. It was adapted for the 2012 documentary *Superthief: Inside America's Biggest Bank Score* and is in development for a motion picture.

To Kill the Irishman: The War That Crippled the Mafia
(Next Hat Press, 1998)
The 2011 motion picture, *Kill the Irishman*, directed by Jonathan Hensleigh and costarring Ray Stevenson, Vincent D'Onofrio, Val Kilmer, and Christopher Walken, was adapted from this book. It is the story of bold Irish American rack-eteer Danny Greene, who took on the Mafia in a 1970s bombing war. Greene has also been the subject of several documentaries in which the author has appeared.

The Rise and Fall of the Cleveland Mafia: Corn Sugar and Blood
(Barricade Books, 1995)
This is the author's first book and was conceived from curiosity about the Prohibition-era killings of his grandfather and three uncles, Mafia leaders who fought the powerful Lonardo family for control of corn sugar, a lucrative bootleg ingredient, in what became known as the Sugar War.

CPSIA information can be obtained
at www.ICGtesting.com
Printed in the USA
JSHW082305171122
33217JS00004B/13

9 780966 250817